Ursula K. Le Guin

WHO WROTE THAT?

LOUISA MAY ALCOTT

JANE AUSTEN

AVI

L. FRANK BAUM

JUDY BLUME,
    SECOND EDITION

BETSY BYARS

MEG CABOT

BEVERLY CLEARY

ROBERT CORMIER

BRUCE COVILLE

ROALD DAHL

CHARLES DICKENS

ERNEST J. GAINES

THEODOR GEISEL

S.E. HINTON

WILL HOBBS

ANTHONY HOROWITZ

STEPHEN KING

URSULA K. LE GUIN

MADELEINE L'ENGLE

GAIL CARSON LEVINE

C.S. LEWIS,
    SECOND EDITION

LOIS LOWRY

ANN M. MARTIN

STEPHENIE MEYER

L.M. MONTGOMERY

PAT MORA

WALTER DEAN MYERS

ANDRE NORTON

SCOTT O'DELL

CHRISTOPHER PAOLINI

BARBARA PARK

KATHERINE PATERSON

GARY PAULSEN

RICHARD PECK

TAMORA PIERCE

DAVID "DAV" PILKEY

EDGAR ALLAN POE

BEATRIX POTTER

PHILIP PULLMAN

MYTHMAKER:
    THE STORY OF
    J.K. ROWLING,
    SECOND EDITION

MAURICE SENDAK

SHEL SILVERSTEIN

LEMONY SNICKET

GARY SOTO

JERRY SPINELLI

R.L. STINE

EDWARD L.
    STRATEMEYER

MARK TWAIN

E.B. WHITE

LAURA INGALLS
    WILDER

LAURENCE YEP

JANE YOLEN

WHO WROTE THAT?

Ursula K. Le Guin

Jeremy K. Brown

Foreword by
Kyle Zimmer

CHELSEA HOUSE
P U B L I S H E R S
An imprint of Infobase Publishing

Ursula K. Le Guin

Chelsea House
An imprint of Infobase Publishing
132 West 31st Street
New York, NY 10001

Library of Congress Cataloging-in-Publication Data
Brown, Jeremy K.
  Ursula K. Le Guin / Jeremy K. Brown.
  p. cm. — (Who wrote that?)
  Includes bibliographical references and index.
  ISBN 978-1-60413-724-8 (hardcover : acid-free paper) 1. Le Guin, Ursula K.,
1929- Juvenile literature. 2. Authors, American—20th century—Biography—Juvenile
literature. 3. Science fiction—Authorship—Juvenile literature. 4. Children's stories—
Authorship—Juvenile literature. I. Title. II. Series.
  PS3562.E42Z57 2010
  813'.54—dc22
  [B]   2010006600

Chelsea House books are available at special discounts when purchased in bulk quantities for business, associations, institutions, or sales promotions. Please call our Special Sales Department in New York at (212) 967-8800 or (800) 322-8755.

You can find Chelsea House on the World Wide Web at http://www.chelseahouse.com.

Text design by Keith Trego
Cover design by Alicia Post
Composition by EJB Publishing Services
Cover printed by Bang Printing, Brainerd, MN
Book printed and bound by Bang Printing, Brainerd, MN
Date printed: November 2010
Printed in the United States of America

10 9 8 7 6 5 4 3 2 1

This book is printed on acid-free paper.

All links and Web addresses were checked and verified to be correct at the time of publication. Because of the dynamic nature of the Web, some addresses and links may have changed since publication and may no longer be valid.

Table of Contents

FOREWORD BY
KYLE ZIMMER
PRESIDENT, FIRST BOOK

HUMANITY IS POWERED by stories. From our earliest days as thinking beings, we employed every available tool to tell each other stories. We danced, drew pictures on the walls of our caves, spoke, and sang. All of this extraordinary effort was designed to entertain, recount the news of the day, explain natural occurrences—and then gradually to build religious and cultural traditions and establish the common bonds and continuity that eventually formed civilizations. Stories are the most powerful force in the universe; they are the primary element that has distinguished our evolutionary path.

Our love of the story has not diminished with time. Enormous segments of societies are devoted to the art of storytelling. Book sales in the United States alone topped $24 billion in 2006; movie studios spend fortunes to create and promote stories; and the news industry is more pervasive in its presence than ever before.

There is no mystery to our fascination. Great stories are magic. They can introduce us to new cultures, or remind us of the nobility and failures of our own, inspire us to greatness or scare us to death; but above all, stories provide human insight on a level that is unavailable through any other source. In fact, stories connect each of us to the rest of humanity not just in our own time, but also throughout history.

This special magic of books is the greatest treasure that we can hand down from generation to generation. In fact, that spark in a child that comes from books became the motivation for the creation of my organization, First Book, a national literacy program with a simple mission: to provide new books to the most disadvantaged children. At present, First Book has been at work in hundreds of communities for over a decade. Every year children in need receive millions of books through our organization and millions more are provided through dedicated literacy institutions across the United States and around the world. In addition, groups of people dedicate themselves tirelessly to working with children to share reading and stories in every imaginable setting from schools to the streets. Of course, this Herculean effort serves many important goals. Literacy translates to productivity and employability in life and many other valid and even essential elements. But at the heart of this movement are people who love stories, love to read, and want desperately to ensure that no one misses the wonderful possibilities that reading provides.

When thinking about the importance of books, there is an overwhelming urge to cite the literary devotion of great minds. Some have written of the magnitude of the importance of literature. Amy Lowell, an American poet, captured the concept when she said, "Books are more than books. They are the life, the very heart and core of ages past, the reason why men lived and worked and died, the essence and quintessence of their lives." Others have spoken of their personal obsession with books, as in Thomas Jefferson's simple statement: "I live for books." But more compelling, perhaps, is the almost instinctive excitement in children for books and stories.

Throughout my years at First Book, I have heard truly extraordinary stories about the power of books in the lives of children. In one case, a homeless child, who had been bounced from one location to another, later resurfaced— and the only possession that he had fought to keep was the book he was given as part of a First Book distribution months earlier. More recently, I met a child who, upon receiving the book he wanted, flashed a big smile and said, "This is my big chance!" These snapshots reveal the true power of books and stories to give hope and change lives.

As these children grow up and continue to develop their love of reading, they will owe a profound debt to those volunteers who reached out to them—a debt that they may repay by reaching out to spark the next generation of readers. But there is a greater debt owed by all of us—a debt to the storytellers, the authors, who have bound us together, inspired our leaders, fueled our civilizations, and helped us put our children to sleep with their heads full of images and ideas.

WHO WROTE THAT? is a series of books dedicated to introducing us to a few of these incredible individuals. While we have almost always honored stories, we have not uniformly honored storytellers. In fact, some of the most important authors have toiled in complete obscurity throughout their lives or have been openly persecuted for the uncomfortable truths that they have laid before us. When confronted with the magnitude of their written work or perhaps the daily grind of our own, we can forget that writers are people. They struggle through the same daily indignities and dental appointments, and they experience the intense joy and bottomless despair that many of us do. Yet somehow they rise above it all to deliver a powerful thread that connects us all. It is a rare honor to have the opportunity that these books provide to share the lives of these extraordinary people. Enjoy.

The critically acclaimed and best-selling American author Ursula K. Le Guin has written novels, poetry, children's books, essays, and short stories. She is best known for her very original and thought-provoking works of fantasy and science fiction.

1

A Strong Voice

IN 1972, URSULA K. LE GUIN was awarded the National Book Award for her novel *The Farthest Shore*, the third book in her wildly popular Earthsea series. Though it was not the first book award she had won, this particular prize was especially meaningful to her. "I also rejoice in the privilege of sharing this honor, if I may, with my fellow writers, not only in the field of children's books, but in that even less respectable field, science fiction," she said in her acceptance speech. "For I am not only a fantasist but a science fiction writer, and odd though it may seem, I am proud to be both."[1]

For nearly a half century, Ursula K. Le Guin has enthralled readers with her novels, short stories, and children's books that tell of far-off worlds with rich histories and extensively detailed cultures, maps, and religions all their own. Not only has she spun whole universes that span several novels, she even holds the distinction of being the first author to create a school for wizards in her books! She has written novels in various genres but has been most at home in science fiction, where she has used the trappings of the style (space travel, alien life, distant worlds) to shed light on real problems affecting our own world. Her books have addressed racism, gender equality, the misuse of power, and topical issues such as the Vietnam War. Although best known for her science fiction, she has often stated that the decision to work in the genre was not a conscious one. "I intended to be a writer, as long as I can remember," she said. "I knew nothing about genres as a child, and cannot say that I chose to write fantasy; I followed my imagination wherever it took me."[2]

INCREDIBLE OUTPUT

An incredibly prolific writer, Le Guin has penned more than 19 novels, published 8 short story collections, and written 6 nonfiction books. Her Earthsea books—chronicling the lives and times of wizards living in a richly detailed archipelago—have been compared to J.R.R. Tolkien's epic fantasy *The Lord of the Rings* and C.S. Lewis' Narnia books—works among the best fantasy novels of all time. And, on top of these accomplishments, Le Guin has also amassed a number of prestigious awards, including four Hugo Awards and two Nebulas, both the top prizes in science fiction writing.

In addition, Ursula K. Le Guin has been a voice for women writers over the years. In a genre long dominated by men, Le Guin has stood out. She has referred to herself as a feminist, although she has also said that the term is not wholly accurate when describing her point of view. "I have frequently described myself as a feminist, because feminist thinking and writing of the '60s and '70s had a huge liberating influence on me," she said, "setting my mind free from a whole lot of masculist bigotries and superstitions; and so it would be untruthful and ungrateful not to call myself a feminist, even if the term doesn't fully describe either my thinking or my writing. . . . Besides, when you say you're a feminist it annoys the bigots . . . and the prissy ladies so much, it's kind of irresistible."[3]

SPEAKING FOR WOMEN

Le Guin has also gone on to say that her advocating for strong female characters and feminist ideals in her books initially came not from a political or activist standpoint, but rather a more straightforward one: "My feminism before the women's movement started consisted simply of the fact that I wasn't going to let any men put me down because I wasn't a man."[4]

Over the years, but particularly when she started out, Le Guin encountered some resistance from male editors. Nevertheless, she often found clever methods of beating

Did you know...

Ursula K. Le Guin has won numerous awards throughout her career for her imaginative writing. With separate wins for both the Hugo and Nebula, Le Guin is the only writer to have won each of these awards more than once!

the system. In one humorous anecdote, Le Guin recalled the hoops she had to jump through when submitting a story to a male-driven publication:

> My agent (a woman) submitted the story as by "U.K. Le Guin," and when the editors found out that I was Ursula, not Ulysses, they asked to keep the initials, "because our readership is frightened by women writers." I said, "There, there, boys, now don't be frightened, it's O.K., I'm U.K." And then they asked me for an autobiographical note! So I wrote: "The stories of U.K. Le Guin are not written by U.K. Le Guin, but by another person of the same name." I figured that might puzzle their readers, but not frighten them.[5]

Above all, Le Guin considers herself to be more than a feminist, anarchist, socialist, or pragmatist. She considers herself to be, quite simply, a writer who wishes to shed light on some of the issues facing our world: "Writing is simply a major part of the way I live . . . like having kids or being a member of a family or cooking meals," she said. "It's one of the things I do. . . . But of course one tries to do it well, and since it's an act of communication, a public act, one is obliged to try to do it well because other people are involved in it. After all, the readers—you owe them an obligation."[6]

In this February 2005 photo, students walk near Sather Tower on the University of California at Berkeley campus in California. Ursula K. Le Guin's father, Alfred L. Kroeber, was a world-famous anthropologist who taught at Berkeley. The university's anthropology department is named in his honor.

2

The Beginning Place

"ALL MY WORK is full of the Western landscape, the hills, the forests, the deserts, the light," Ursula Kroeber Le Guin once remarked. "In my books, the sun always sets in the ocean."[1] Indeed, having lived her entire life on the West Coast of the United States, it is not surprising that it has had a major influence on her writing. Le Guin was born on October 21, 1929, in Berkeley, California, the daughter of the renowned anthropologist Alfred Louis Kroeber and the writer Theodora Kroeber (formerly Kracaw). "I was the fourth, and only girl, and welcomed as such by parents and brothers," she recalled.

Rather fragile as a baby, then became quite solid. Obedient, bright, a good girl. Too shy to play or talk with anyone at school until about fifth grade, when I made a couple of friends. My parents and brothers were spirited, kindly, loving, highly intelligent people; my microcosm was a sweet one.[2]

Kroeber and his wife had achieved some fame during the early part of the twentieth century for their documentation of a man named Ishi, who was believed to be the last Native American in California. Kroeber first met Ishi after Ishi had been taken into custody by a sheriff in the small mining town of Oroville. From there he was moved to the University of California at Berkeley, where he remained for the rest of his life. At Berkeley, Kroeber studied Ishi extensively, even giving him his name. Theodora used her husband's notes to publish two books on Ishi, *Ishi in Two Worlds* (1961) and *Ishi: The Last of His Tribe* (1964). Ishi's story and Ursula's father's work as an anthropologist would have a strong influence on young Ursula. "My father studied real cultures and I make them up—in a way, it's the same thing,"[3] she said later.

From her mother, Ursula inherited independence and her strong sense of feminism. Years later, when writing the introduction to a new edition of her mother's novel *The Inland Whale*, she wrote:

Did you know...

Ursula K. Le Guin's first name comes from St. Ursula, a British Christian saint whose feast day, October 21, is the same as the author's birthday. St. Ursula is the patron saint of archers, orphans, and students.

From her mother Phebe and other strong women of her late-frontier Western childhood, Theodora had a firm heritage of female independence and self-respect. . . . She made her daughter feel a lifelong welcome, giving me the conviction that I had done the right thing in being born a woman—a gift many woman-children are denied.[4]

Overall, Le Guin has credited her father for having the most direct influence on her becoming a writer. "My mother didn't write anything 'til she was getting on to 60, so I guess it had to be my father," she said. "But I didn't read much of what he wrote until I was in my 30s, so his influence must have been osmotic. Also genetic—I believe my mind works somewhat the way his did, though less disciplined and methodical. He loved to read fantasy, by the way."[5]

SUMMER GETAWAYS

Ursula's family spent the bulk of the year living in the university town of Berkeley, California, but during the summer, they lived at Kishamish, a 40-acre (16.2 hectare) farm in the lush, tranquil Napa Valley, 60 miles (96.7 kilometers) north of San Francisco. The farm was a place in which the Kroeber children fashioned their own world: A field would become a makeshift baseball diamond, an irrigation tank was converted into a swimming pool, and the redwood barn was a place to put on plays (performed by the Barntop Players of Kishamish). Writing in her book *Alfred Kroeber: A Personal Configuration*, Theodora Kroeber recalled her children's explorations of the land around Kishamish:

As they learned the old trails or made new ones . . . the children ranged farther and farther afield. From the floor of the valley to the top of St. John is open land broken by small streams and by canyons, brushy or tree-covered. You could ride or hike for hours encountering only a squatter and his family occupying a deserted farmhouse, one or two deer fences, and the remnant

Did you know...

Alfred Louis Kroeber, Ursula K. Le Guin's father, was one of the most famous anthropologists the world has ever known. He helped to move anthropology from the fringes of science into the respected position it holds today. Over the course of his distinguished career, Kroeber held five honorary degrees (from Yale, Harvard, Columbia, the University of California, and the University of Chicago) and was an honorary member of no less than 16 different scientific societies.

After graduating college in 1896 with a degree in English and receiving his master's in Romantic Drama, Kroeber attended Columbia University, where his 28-page dissertation on the art of the Arapaho Indians earned him one of the first 12 doctorates in anthropology ever awarded by the university. After earning his degree, Kroeber settled in at the University of California at Berkeley, where he was a professor of anthropology and the director of the California Museum of Anthropology. During this period, Kroeber met Ishi, who was possibly the last Native American in California. Kroeber's studies of Ishi helped open the world's eyes to the history and culture of Native Americans in the region.

Alfred Kroeber died in Paris on October 5, 1960, at 84 years old. Today, the headquarters of UC Berkeley's anthropology department is known as Kroeber Hall. In 1992, he was portrayed on film by actor Jon Voight in the movie *The Last of His Tribe*.

trees of an orchard beside the cellar of a former house. For the rest, there was silence, broken by the rustle of deer and smaller brush animals and birds.[6]

Kishamish was, as Kroeber wrote, "a world without phones or doorbells or the tyranny of close schedules; a world for exploration, for reading, for one's own work, for swimming and playing games, for sitting by the outdoor fire until late in the night, talking, telling stories, singing; for sleeping under the stars."[7]

A HOUSE FULL OF CHARACTERS

In addition, the family summer home was often filled with visitors, ranging from Native Americans to writers, scholars, and professors from Europe. In an interview with Scott Timberg for the *Los Angeles Times*, Le Guin recalled her vibrant childhood. "I was privileged," she told the writer, "to know the kind of people that most American kids, most bourgeois white kids, don't."[8]

Reading and storytelling were also a vital part of life in the Kroeber household. Stories ranging from classical literature to Native American folklore were read, passed down, or told over campfires. "My parents both read all the time," she said, "my father wrote all the time (when he wasn't teaching), and the house was full of books; reading and writing were constant, natural activities and pleasures, pretty much like eating and breathing."[9] Some of Le Guin's earliest memories were of stories and storytelling. She remembered:

Listening to my mother read *The Swiss Family Robinson* to my older brothers and trying hard to stay awake. Listening to my great-aunt Betsy talk about her life in Wyoming and Colorado and tell stories about the family while she ironed and cooked and I hung around. Listening to my father tell northern California Indian stories at the campfire on summer nights in the Napa Valley. I think he was mentally translating some of them as he told them. The telling voice was very quiet and a little hesitant. Listening through the wall between our rooms to my brother Karl telling himself heroic sagas of his own invention, with a lot of bangs and "Take that!"s in them.[10]

Ursula and her brothers, Karl, Ted, and Clifton, were not only enamored with the reading, telling, or hearing of stories, they enjoyed *acting* them out as well. "I was one of the Belgae attacking Caesar's camp (on a hill in California), about ten years before I ever read Caesar," she said.

We got into a little trouble because of the catapult we built, which hurled large rocks quite efficiently. Later on, Karl was Robin Hood and I was Little John . . . "Have at thee, varlet!" We got into a little trouble because of the quarterstaff combats. As my father pointed out, a quarterstaff can be a deadly weapon—though not often when wielded by nine-year-olds.[11]

FIRST STORIES

In addition to recreating her favorite stories, Ursula became interested in writing some on her own. She decided to submit her first story to *Astounding Science Fiction*, a popular magazine of the era. She and her brother had been reading that publication, as well as similar magazines in the genre, and the quality of the stories gave her confidence. "I thought, I write better than some of this stuff. So I wrote a modest story involving a time machine and the origin of life, and submitted it. It came back with a polite rejection letter, of which I was rightly proud."[12]

Initially, Ursula was not a fan of the sci-fi or fantasy genres. "When I was about 11," she said, "my brother and I used to buy *Astounding* [and other pulps]. We sneered at a lot of it. We were pretty arrogant kids."[13] Despite her initial resistance to sci-fi and fantasy, these soon became her preferred genres, inspired in no small part by the works of the Anglo-Irish author Lord Dusany (the pen name of the eighteenth Baron of Dusany, Edward Plunkett). At 12 years old, Ursula had read Dusany's novel *A Dreamer's Tales* and was instantly captivated. The book's first paragraph tells of three mysterious regions—Toldees, Mondath, and Arizim—that are known collectively as the Inner Lands. Dusany goes into great detail describing this fantastical world:

> Toldees, Mondath, Arizim, these are the Inner Lands, the lands whose sentinels upon their borders do not behold the sea. Beyond them to the east there lies a desert, for ever untroubled by man: all yellow it is, and spotted with shadows of stones, and Death is in it, like a leopard lying in the sun. To the south they are bounded by magic, to the west by a mountain.[14]

These words immediately captivated Ursula and shaped her own writing style. "What I hadn't realized, I guess, is that people were still making up myths," she later observed. "One made up stories oneself, of course; but here was a grownup doing it, for grownups, without a single apology to common sense, without an explanation, just dropping us straight into the Inner Lands. Whatever the reason, the moment was decisive. I had discovered my native country."[15]

In 1951, Ursula K. Le Guin earned her undergraduate degree at Radcliffe College in Cambridge, Massachusetts. At this historically all-female school, she studied French and Italian Renaissance literature.

3

From California to Paris

AT SCHOOL, URSULA continued to foster her interest in writing, focusing mainly on poetry. "I had good teachers in the Berkeley schools but was too shy and introverted to let them befriend me," she said. "Josephine Miles, a poet who taught at UC Berkeley, was most gentle and encouraging to me when my mother encouraged me to show her some of my poems at about age fourteen. She was a great, beloved teacher of poetry. She took me seriously and so helped take my writing seriously."[1]

As Ursula grew out of her teenage years, still writing and creating, she began to reshape a lot of her views on the world and take a mature worldview concerning politics, feminism, and culture. These views would go on to impact her speculative fiction, which have often served as metaphors for the things that were happening in the world. "At sixteen, seventeen, eighteen years old I worked hard at figuring out my personal responsibility for what I did with my highly privileged life and realized that this moral responsibility was also political . . . and I guess I felt that to undertake such responsibilities was to be grownup—a burden, an honor."[2]

In 1947, Ursula went to Radcliffe College, an all-women's institution and then-sister school to Harvard University, in Cambridge, Massachusetts. At Radcliffe, she focused her studies on French and Italian in Renaissance literature, eventually receiving her Bachelor of Arts degree in Romance languages in 1951.

VISITING ORSINIA

After graduating Radcliffe, Ursula moved to New York to begin her graduate studies at Columbia University. During this time, she also invented Orsinia, a fictional Central European country that would be the setting for many of her early stories. The name Orsinia has its roots in the Italian word *orsino*, or "bearish," and the name Ursula comes from *ursa*, the Latin word for "bear," so, as Le Guin later explained, "it's my country so it bears my name."[3] The stories she wrote about Orsinia were an important step forward in her finding her own voice as a writer.

After graduating Columbia with her master's degree in 1952, Ursula was awarded a Fulbright scholarship, and she boarded a ship for Paris to continue her studies. Aboard the *Queen Mary*, she met historian and fellow Fulbright scholar Charles A. Le Guin. They fell in love almost immediately and were married on Christmas Day, 1953.

The exterior of Columbia University in New York City as it looked in the early 1950s when Ursula K. Le Guin was attending the school. At Columbia she earned her master's degree as well as a Fulbright scholarship, which allowed her to continue her studies in Paris, France.

Upon returning to America, the Le Guins moved to Macon, Georgia, where Ursula Le Guin took a job as a French professor at Mercer University. During this time, she also had been preparing her doctoral thesis on the

French poet Jean Lemaire de Belges but soon cut short her work when their first child, Elisabeth, was born in 1957. "I realized, kind of painfully, and much against my father's will, that I didn't need a doctorate any more," she said.

> I had married one. We didn't need two in the family. I had been getting my doctorate in order to support my habit—writing. My father had been strong on this. He said, "You know, if you want to be a free writer, you've got to be financially independent." He was sad that I had got that far and then stopped.[4]

Being a full-time mother might have curtailed Le Guin's academic pursuits, but it did not stop her from indulging her greatest passion: writing. In fact, Le Guin has stated that balancing work and family life was always an important belief shared by her and her husband. "It was tough trying to keep writing while bringing up three kids, but my husband was totally in it with me, and so it worked out fine," she said. "Le Guins' Rule: One person cannot do two fulltime jobs, but two persons can do three fulltime jobs—if they honestly share the work. The idea that you

Did you know...

When Ursula K. Le Guin's children were younger, the only free time she could find to write was at night after everyone had gone to sleep. She would often begin at 9 p.m. and write as long as she could stay awake. Once her children grew older and went to school, she wrote during the day until they came home. Nowadays, her writing routine often begins in the morning and ends sometime in the early afternoon.

need an ivory tower to write in, that if you have babies you can't have books, that artists are somehow exempt from the dirty work of life—rubbish."[5]

In the mid-1950s, while living in Georgia, Le Guin came across J.R.R. Tolkien's three-volume fantasy epic *The Lord of the Rings*, and was instantly transfixed:

> I had been resisting the books with their red-and-black staring-eye covers and fulsome reviews in the *Saturday Review*. I was suspicious. But one day at the Emory University Library, having nothing to read, I picked up the first volume and took it home. Next day I hurried to the library in terrible fear that somebody might have checked out the other two volumes. I got them, and my memory is that I read them in three days, which really is not possible, even for careless galloping readers like me, is it? Anyhow, thereafter, Middle Earth has been one of the great kingdoms of this world to me, and I have gone back to it, as often as to *War and Peace*, I suppose. I am grateful that I was in my twenties when I first read Tolkien and had gone far enough towards finding my own voice and way as a writer that I could learn from him (endlessly) without being overwhelmed, overinfluenced by him.[6]

By 1961, at which point the Le Guin's second child, Caroline, had joined the family, Le Guin had completed five novels, most of them set in the fictional world of Orsinia. She eagerly submitted them to various publishers and agents, all of whom returned the manuscripts to her, deeming them "too remote." On the subject of their remoteness, Le Guin has stated that she agrees. "Searching for a technique of distancing, I had come upon this one," she later wrote.

> Unfortunately, it was not a technique used by anybody at the moment. . . . You must either fit a category, or "have a name,"

to publish a book in America. As the only way I was ever going to achieve namehood was *by* writing, I was reduced to fitting into a category. Therefore my first efforts to write science fiction were motivated by a pretty distinct wish to get published.[7]

RETURN TO SCIENCE FICTION

Perhaps Le Guin's first realization that she could write the kind of stories she wanted to in the science fiction genre was when she read the work of Cordwainer Smith. Smith was the pseudonym for Paul Linebarger, a professor, military intelligence expert, and member of the Foreign Policy Association. When Le Guin first came upon Smith's short story "Alpha Ralpha Boulevard," it reignited her interest in science fiction. "I don't really remember what I thought when I read it," she recalled, "but what I think now I ought to have thought when I read it is, *My God! It can be done!*"[8]

Inspired by Smith's work, Le Guin began composing science fiction stories. Her initial forays back into the genre were somewhat rocky. In her 1979 essay "A Citizen of Mondath," Le Guin recalls that transition:

> The shift from the kind of writing I had done before to categorizable "fantasy" and "science fiction" was not a big one, but I had a good deal to learn all the same. Also I was pretty ignorant of science, and was just beginning to educate myself (a hopeless job, but one which I continue to enjoy immensely). At first I knew too little science to use it as a framework, as part of the essential theme, of a story, and so wrote fairy tales decked out in space suits.[9]

Le Guin's first story to be published was "April in Paris," which appeared in *Fantastic Stories of Imagination* in

1962. The story uses the author's knowledge of the French Renaissance period to create a tale of a sixteenth century scientist who turns to magic after losing faith in science. While trying a spell, he conjures a scholar from the twentieth century and the two become friends.

Le Guin's next story, "The Masters," delved further into the realm of science fiction, telling the story of Genil, a man who has learned all he is permitted to in a land where science is considered to be heresy. Genil's curiosity regarding numbers and mathematics soon lands him in terrible trouble. In the early 1960s, she published several other stories, including "Darkness Box," "The World of Unbinding," and "The Rule of Names." These last two stories served as preludes to the Earthsea series.

In 1964, *Amazing Fact and Science Fiction* published "The Dowry of Angyar" (later known as "Semley's Necklace"). The story tells of Semley, the wife of a nobleman on the planet Fomalhaut II who embarks upon a quest for a gold and sapphire necklace that is an heirloom of her family. Against the counsel of her peers, Semley leaves her castle to search for it. Her journey eventually leads her to the Clayfolk, a race of interstellar beings whose constituents whisk Semley to another planet. There she meets Rocannon, an ethnologist (or person who studies different cultures) who bequeaths to her the necklace she has been searching for. However, upon returning to her own world, Semley discovers that 16 years have passed. Distraught, she gives the necklace to her now-grown daughter and leaves the castle forever. This story served as a precursor to Le Guin's first published novel, *Rocannon's World*. After years of publishing only poetry and short fiction, Ursula K. Le Guin's world was about to change.

By the time this picture was taken in 1985, Ursula K. Le Guin was considered one of science fiction's leading authors. Among her best-known science fiction works is the Hainish Cycle series, which explores various anthropological and sociological ideas on far-off worlds. The series gets its name from the planet Hain. Hundreds of thousands of years ago, the people of Hain colonized a large number of worlds, including Earth.

4

The Cycle Begins

FOR URSULA K. LE GUIN, "The Dowry of Angyar" was more than just another published short story, it was a gateway to another world. With her next work, *Rocannon's World* (1966), she passed through that gate and so created what is now known as the Hainish Cycle of books and stories.

Taking their cue from the tales and legends of Norse mythology, the Hainish Cycle (also known as the Novels of the Ekumen) takes place approximately three centuries from now and covers more than 2,500 years of future history. The series has gone on to encompass eight novels and 13 short stories. Yet creating an entire universe was never Le Guin's intention at the beginning, which explains why many fans have pointed out inconsistencies in the books. "I didn't set out to write a series, exactly," she told Guy Haley in *Death Ray*.

> It just grew, like Topsy in *Uncle Tom's Cabin*. I found it a lot easier to keep going back to the same universe than to keep making up new ones. Ask God—God probably doesn't forget what he did with various places and peoples, though. I do. So people who try to make a grand history out of the Hainish books are doomed to extreme frustration—they find whole millennia missing, two planets with the same name—Werel— that aren't the same planet—a universe of boo-boos. It's such a mess you'd think Coyote [the Native American Trickster god] made it. Like this one.[1]

The first novel in the series, *Rocannon's World*, reacquaints readers with Rocannon, a minor but pivotal character from "The Dowry of Angyar." In fact, that story serves as the novel's prologue. Looking back, Le Guin has acknowledged that *Rocannon*'s roots are found in "The Dowry of Angyar." In that parable, she notes, she found "the germ of a novel."[2] The character of Rocannon suddenly went from bit player to major character, as if he himself stood up and demanded that he be recognized. "I'm Rocannon," Le Guin quoted her creation as saying, "I want to explore my world."[3]

The story begins as Gaveral Rocannon embarks on a mission to Semley's world of Fomalhaut II, long after the events of the prologue, accompanied by Semley's grandchild, Mogien. The assignment is a peaceful one, as Rocannon is planning to simply conduct an ethnological survey of Fomalhaut II. Then his ship is destroyed by an enemy race, the Faraday, that has established a base on the planet. The remainder of the novel follows Rocannon as he makes his way to the Faraday installation with help from the locals. Along his journey, he encounters many strange and unusual lands and travels on the back of the winged felines known as "windsteeds." Rocannon's travels eventually take him to a cave where he meets an ancient life-form that grants him the ability of telepathy (which Le Guin dubs "mindspeech"). With his new gift, Rocannon is able to hear the thoughts of his enemies and use that knowledge to send a faster-than-light ship to destroy them. The novel ends with a flash forward nine years into the future. A rescue party arrives to find that Rocannon has died a loved and respected lord of this world, which has now been named for him.

Rocannon's World represented a great leap forward for Le Guin, one that allowed her to create a wholly invented world, complete with a culture and customs entirely its own. The book also gave her the freedom to utilize her love of myths and legend, specifically Norse mythology. In the book, the elfish race known as the Fiia refer to Rocannon as the Wanderer, a name also given to Odin, the greatest god in the Norse pantheon and the ruler of Asgard, the home of the Norse gods.

In one passage of the novel, Rocannon is captured by a group of peasants. They tie Rocannon to a post and attempt to burn him, but his futuristic garb renders him impervious to the flames. Eventually, he is set free by one of the disobedient servants and walks freely from the camp. In her biography *Ursula K. Le Guin*, Barbara J. Bucknall notes how these events parallel the famous fables of Odin, as retold by the Irish folklorist Padraic Colum. In the tale, she notes:

> Odin came to the hall of a king, Geirrod, . . . who has become the leader of a band of robbers. To test him, Odin requested hospitality and was badly treated. Told to sing, Odin sang a song reproaching Geirrod, and as punishment, was tied to one of the pillars of the hall with a fire lit under him. Odin was quite unharmed by the fire, but the cruel king kept him bound for nine nights. The servants were forbidden to bring him food or drink, but Gierrod's gentle brother, Agat, brought Odin a horn of ale every morning at dawn. On the ninth night, Odin denounced Geirrod, freed himself from his chains and turned Geirrod and his followers into wild beasts.[4]

NEW WORLDS, NEW TECHNOLOGY

Rocannon's World also demonstrated Le Guin's creativity when imagining new worlds and the creatures, people, and devices that make them up. For example, in the novel, Rocannon attempts to contact his world using a communication mechanism known as an ansible. Le Guin created the term to describe a machine that could transmit messages across galactic space instantaneously, and it has since become a commonly used term in science fiction, having appeared in works by Orson Scott Card, Verner Vinge, and L.A. Graf. Card, in particular, has made extensive use of the ansible, making it a significant part of his groundbreaking novel *Ender's Game*. In the novel, the device is referred to as the Philotic Parallax Instantaneous Communicator. A clever nod to the creator of the term comes when someone refers to the name ansible as having been "dredged out of an old book somewhere and it caught on."

Ursula K. Le Guin is credited with the creation of the "ansible," a hypothetical device that is capable of near instantaneous communication between two points in interstellar space. Ansibles have been used in a number of science fiction novels and stories, including the works of Orson Scott Card, who is best known for his novel **Ender's Game.**

The use of the ansible is one example of how Le Guin has fashioned technology completely out of her imagination in order to suit the purposes of the story. It has become something of a trademark for her, a fact which pleases her greatly. She also says that, given the chance to redo her books, she would not change a thing. "The ansible works fine, doesn't it?" she said to Guy Haley.

> Most of the fundamental tropes of science fiction—zooming around the galaxy at FTL (Faster Than Light) speeds or via strings or whatever, meeting and communicating with aliens on other planets, interplanetary wars and empires with leagues, all that—it's pure hokum. Pure and glorious. The space ship is not a prediction, it's a metaphor. That doesn't invalidate it! Just the opposite; it makes it as useful as it is enjoyable.[5]

Following *Rocannon's World*, Le Guin remained in the Hainish realm with her next novel, *Planet of Exile*. The book, which is not a sequel, tells the tale of a distant planet, Werel, on the verge of a 15-year winter. As the cold season approaches, the Tevarians, one of the two races that inhabit Werel, are preparing by building a fortified winter city. Into this city comes Jakob Agat, an Earthman who has been marooned on this world. He warns the Tevarians of the coming of the Gaal, Werel's other inhabitants. The Gaal are plundering cities in the hopes of building a kingdom of their own. Wold, the Teverian chief, and his daughter, Rolery, soon join with Jakob and battle the Gaal.

Planet of Exile is significant in Le Guin's bibliography, as the character of Rolery shows a woman who is strong-willed and able to stand alongside the men with equal, if not greater, strength of character. She also is a woman who stands apart from her culture by her choice to marry the Earthman, Jakob Agat. "Rolery, a young and inexperienced woman of a rigidly traditional, male-supremacist culture, does not fight, or initiate sexual encounters, or become a leader of society, or assume any role which, in her culture or ours of 1964, could be labeled 'male,'" Le Guin said.

> She is, however, a rebel, both socially and sexually. Although her behavior is not aggressive, her desire for freedom drives her to break right out of her culture-mold: she changes herself entirely by allying herself with an alien self. She chooses the Other. This small personal rebellion, coming at a crucial time, initiates events which lead to the complete changing and remaking of two cultures and societies.[6]

In addition to examining gender roles, *Planet of Exile* also delves into very complex issues about societies, race, and cultural differences. For example, the colonists (Jakob's people) refer to the native Werelians as "hilfs," a term which means Highly Intelligent Life Forms, while the native people think of the Earth people as witches, because of their advanced technology and different customs and ways. Although not explicitly cruel or hurtful, the words still serve to divide the two cultures, preventing them from being truly united. Only at the end of the great battle do all agree to no longer use the words and simply refer to one another as men and women. The theme of differences between cultures is further touched upon when Rolery (who is white) and Jakob (who is darker-skinned) touch hands, symbolizing, in Le Guin's words, "the salute of equals."

As in *Rocannon's World*, *Planet of Exile* touches on the characters' extrasensory abilities in the form of "mindspeech," the Le Guin equivalent of mental telepathy. Jakob, a member of the League of All Worlds, is skilled at speaking with only his mind, and he does so when he first encounters Rolery. Although her species is not able to use mindspeech, Rolery and Jakob nevertheless can communicate without words. In this, Le Guin creates a metaphor for love and marriage, in which two people do not need to speak to understand what the other is thinking or feeling. This concept of love and true communication between beings is a major theme that appears often in her books.

Le Guin followed *Planet of Exile* with *City of Illusions* in 1967. This novel, though still part of the Hainish series, was different, as it was not set on a far-off planet but on Earth of the very distant future. The story concerns a man with no memory who is found by villagers living in what once was the eastern region of North America. The man, who the villagers name Falk, has the appearance of a human but also possesses strange, alien eyes that make him appear almost catlike. For readers of *Planet of Exile*, this should be an immediate tipoff as to Falk's true identity, as the catlike eyes were a distinctive character trait of Rolery and her people.

Falk lives with the villagers for a half-dozen years, learning their ways and absorbing stories about the Shing, a race of beings who are the present-day rulers of the planet. It is these beings that Falk hopes to meet when he sets out for the mountains in the west to learn the secret of his identity. He is in search of Es Toch, the hidden base of the Shing.

Arriving at Es Toch, Falk meets Orry, a boy who, it turns out, had traveled to this world with Falk. He calls Falk by his true name, Agad Ramarren, and explains that they are travelers from the planet Werel (the setting for *Planet of Exile*) who were ambushed in an attack by the men who are native to this world. It was in this attack that Falk had his memory erased. The Shing claim to be benevolent life forms and offer Falk the chance to restore his memories. Falk, however, suspects that the Shing were the ones who attacked him, erased his memories, and left him abandoned in the forest. Furthermore, Falk believes that they desire to read his mind in order to learn the location of Werel. Regardless, Falk agrees to the procedure and his old personality is restored, and with it, a greater knowledge of his life prior to the attack. He is also able to fuse his two personalities together, becoming a distinctly new individual. It is when this fusion occurs that Falk is able to deduce the true deceptive nature of the Shing and fight to make his escape. Having two minds (Falk and Ramarren) gives Falk the ability to manipulate the Shing's minds to do his bidding. He uses this gift to mentally overpower a Shing and steal a spaceship. Falk, Orry, and the captured Shing then

Did you know...

The Hainish Cycle is named after Hain, a fictional planet 140 light years from Earth that plays an important role in Le Guin's novels and short stories. Hain is the oldest culture in both the League of Worlds and later the Ekumen. The Hainish people cannot be distinguished from human beings on Earth and helped to seed all of the planets that became part of the Ekumen.

set off for Werel to prepare the liberation of Earth from the rule of their oppressors.

According to Le Guin, *City of Illusions* was inspired by an idea she had of a man with two minds, to be titled *The Two-Minded Man*. The finished book, however, was markedly different and the manuscript was re-titled by someone at the publisher's office. Looking back on the book, Le Guin has complained:

> The Shing are the least convincing lot of people I ever wrote. It came of trying to obey my elder daughter's orders. Elisabeth at eight came and said, "I thought of some people named Shing, you ought to write a story about them." "What are they like?" I asked and she said, with a divine smile and shining eyes, "They're *bad*."—Well, I fluffed it. A troop of little Hitlers from Outer Space; the guys in the black hats. I should have made Elisabeth tell me how to do it. She could have, too. Eight-year-olds know what bad is. Grownups get confused.[7]

Of all her books, *City of Illusions* is Le Guin's least favorite. Over the years, she has been known to speak rather harshly about the novel, saying in an interview, "If I might say so, *City of Illusions* is rather a bad book to use for anything; it's my least favorite and certainly the one with the most just plain stupid mistakes and holes in it."[8] Yet in spite of her rather harsh criticisms, she has also expressed gratitude for the novel because it allowed her to do some new and exciting things as a writer: "Some things I am grateful to this book for: The chance to argue inconclusively with the slogan 'reverence for life,' which by leaving out too much lets the lie get in and eat the apple rotten; The chance to give Rolery and Jakob Agat a descendant; The chance to begin and end a book with darkness, like a dream."

Having finished *City of Illusions*, Le Guin briefly left the Hainish world behind and set her sights on creating a new universe, one that would profoundly impact her life for years to come.

This aerial image shows the Isles of Scilly, off Cornwall, England. Some time after writing her Earthsea fantasy series, Ursula K. Le Guin visited these islands and realized that they were exactly the sort of setting she had pictured for her imaginary world.

5

Earthsea Rising

FIRST PUBLISHED IN 1968, *A Wizard of Earthsea* remains one of Ursula K. Le Guin's best known and most loved novels. It has been favorably compared to J.R.R. Tolkien's *The Lord of the Rings* and has inspired two movie adaptations. Some have even claimed that it inspired J.K. Rowling to create her Harry Potter novels. Yet perhaps the most intriguing thing about it is that it happened almost by chance.

Following the publication of *City of Illusions*, the publishers at Parnassus Press approached Le Guin to create a book that would appeal to older children, giving her complete creative freedom to do it. "Nobody until then had ever asked me to write anything; I had just done so, relentlessly," she said. "To be asked to do it was a great boon. The exhilaration carried me over my apprehensions about writing 'for young people,' something I had never seriously tried."[1]

Upon accepting the assignment, Le Guin immediately turned her thoughts to what to write about. "For some weeks or months I let my imagination go groping around in search of what was wanted, in the dark,"[2] she recalled. In time, Le Guin thought back to two stories she had published earlier. The first, "The Word of Unbinding," concerned a wizard whose only means of escaping his enemy is to die and confront him in the afterlife. She said:

> I don't recall now whether the fact is made much of in the story, but it was perfectly clear in my mind that it took place on an island, one among many islands. I did not give much attention to the setting, as it was . . . not relevant; and developed only such rules of magic as were germane to the very small point the very minor story made.[3]

The other piece of writing Le Guin turned to was "The Rule of Names," which had been published in *Fantastic* some years before. The story also took place on an island, and dealt with the notion that someone who knows the true name of a person or thing then has power over that person or thing. These both would become key themes in the world of *A Wizard of Earthsea*.

Also in the years before writing the first story that took place in Earthsea, she penned another unpublished story about a prince who makes a journey to the other islands in the archipelago that makes up his homeland and encounters a group of people living in a raft colony. "This story wasn't submitted for publication as it never worked itself out at all well," she noted, "but I felt strongly that the basic image—the raft-colony—was a lulu, and would find itself its home somewhere eventually."[4]

When considering what to write for this new book, Le Guin thought back to the islands she had written about in her previous stories, as well as the concept of magic and its various uses. As she went over "The Word of Unbinding," Le Guin began to think of wizards and how they came to be. She imagined that, before becoming all-powerful, these wizards would have to learn about magic, spells, and the

---

Did you know...

Initially, the landscape for Earthsea existed only in Ursula K. Le Guin's mind. She did not picture any specific place while creating it. However, years later, while on a trip to the British Isles, she sailed past the Isles of Scilly, an archipelago off the south-western tip of Great Britain. Looking at the islands from her boat, she realized they looked exactly like the world of Earthsea! "There they were, my islands," she later wrote, "scattered out before us in a golden sea, fantastic, unearthly, surely full of drag-ons: the Scillies."* Since then, she has often told her fans that if they want to see what Earthsea might look like, they should visit the Isles of Scilly.

*"Chronicles of Earthsea," *Guardian* (London), February 9, 2004. http://www.guardian.co.uk/books/2004/feb/09/sciencefictionfantasyand horror.ursulakleguin.

mysterious tricks of their trade. "Serious consideration of magic, and of writing for kids, combined to make me wonder about wizards," said Le Guin. "Wizards are usually elderly or ageless Gandalfs, quite rightly and archetypically. But what were they before they had white beards? How did they learn what is obviously an erudite and dangerous art? Are there colleges for young wizards? And so on."[5] This line of thinking led Le Guin to create a wizarding school, located on the island of Roke, one of many interconnected islands that form the archipelago of Earthsea, where the book's action takes place.

In creating the world of Earthsea, Le Guin has stated that she did not set out with a plan for the world in which her book would take place. Rather, she says, she came upon it, as though it were a real place. "I did not deliberately invent Earthsea," she said. "I did not think 'Hey wow—islands are archetypes, and archipelagoes are superarchetypes and let's build us an archipelago!' I am not an engineer, but an explorer. I discovered Earthsea."[6]

A Wizard of Earthsea tells of the coming of age of a young boy who learns that he is capable of performing magic. As a boy, he is raised under the name Duny, and grows up with no mother and an emotionally distant father. His aunt, a witch in Duny's village, teaches him magic, but she soon learns that his power is greater than hers, so much so that she finds herself frightened by the extent of his power. From his aunt, Duny learns the true names of the various local birds (a thematic nod to "The Rule of Names") and uses his naming of them to call them to him. This notion of having power over the things one has named was something Le Guin found intriguing in her earliest days as a writer. "It's a very old idea in magic, all over the world," she told the London *Guardian* in an online chat.

"I read Lady Frazier's *Leaves from the Golden Bough* as a kid, and probably met it there. Or almost anywhere. A writer, an artist whose medium is words, is likely to find the idea of magic as naming, words as power, a quite natural one."[7]

When Duny's village comes under attack from invaders from the nearby Kargard Empire, the young boy uses a spell to repel the invasion. After the incident brings him fame, he is contacted by a great wizard named Ogion the Silent, who calls Duny by his true name, Ged, and takes him to the school for wizards to begin his proper training.

NAMES IN EARTHSEA

Ged's name, as well as the names of other characters and places in the world of Earthsea, was very important to Le Guin. As previously mentioned, one of the key themes of the Earthsea saga was the idea that knowing someone or something's name was to have power over it. With that in mind, Le Guin took great care in naming her protagonist:

> I worked (in collaboration with a wizard named Ogion) for a long time trying to "listen for" his name, and making certain it really was his name. This all sounds very mystical and indeed there are aspects of it I do not understand, but it is a pragmatic business too, since if the name had been wrong the character would have been wrong—misbegotten, misunderstood.[8]

So important was it to her that her character be properly named that, once the right name had been selected, she did not change it, even when confronted by a misunderstanding with her publisher. "A man who read the [manuscript] for Parnassus thought 'Ged' was meant to suggest 'God,'" she recalled. "I considered changing the name in case there were other such ingenious minds waiting to pounce. But

Did you know...

A young boy who learns he is capable of magic and sent to a school for wizards? While this may sound like another series you know well, Ursula K. Le Guin was writing about wizarding schools long before J.K. Rowling's Harry Potter picked up his first broomstick. Since the publication of the first book in the Harry Potter series, *Harry Potter and the Sorcerer's Stone*, in 1997, Le Guin has had to field a variety of questions from fans and journalists who have noted similarities between the two series. But those who are looking for a furious debate between the two authors, or a snippy reaction from Le Guin, might be disappointed. She told the London *Guardian*, "When so many adult critics were carrying on about the 'incredible originality' of the first Harry Potter book, I read it to find out what the fuss was about, and remained somewhat puzzled; it seemed a lively kid's fantasy crossed with a 'school novel,' good fare for its age group, but stylistically ordinary, imaginatively derivative, and ethically rather mean-spirited."[*]

As for those who have gone so far as to accuse Rowling of blatantly plagiarizing Le Guin's work, the author also remains unfazed. "It's great that so many people have enjoyed her fantasies and thereby rediscovered the genre," Le Guin said to Lev Grossman in an interview. "I could wish she'd been a little more generous about admitting influences, but so what. A lot of borrowing always goes on in an active, vital art form, not plagiarism, just learning from each other. No harm in saying so."[**]

[*] "Chronicles of Earthsea." *Guardian* (London), February 9, 2004. http://www.guardian.co.uk/books/2004/feb/09/sciencefiction fantasyandhorror.ursulakleguin.

[**] Lev Grossman, "An Interview with Ursula K. Le Guin," Techland, May 11, 2009. http://techland.com/2009/05/11/an-interview-with-ursula-k-le-guin.

I couldn't do so. The fellow's name was Ged and no two ways about it."[9]

Under Ogion's training, Ged learns to better manage his powers, although he occasionally allows his overconfidence to get him into trouble. While studying a spell to raise the dead, for example, Ged's curiosity gets the better of him and he performs the spell. Instantly, the room goes dark and Ged becomes aware of a shadow crouching by the door. At that moment, Ogion returns and banishes the shadow-spirit with his staff.

When he arrives at the school for wizards, Ged is still haunted by the shadow seen at Ogion's house, which seems to follow him wherever he goes. Nevertheless, he delves into his studies. Unfortunately, Ged continues to be arrogant and prideful regarding his magical abilities. This egotism results in his casting a dangerous spell that awakens an angry female spirit as well as a stronger version of the shadow-spirit that he had previously summoned, which claws at Ged's face, wounding him. The spell is broken by the head of the school, a man named Archmage Nemmerle, but the act drains him of all his strength and he dies.

The death of Nemmerle haunts Ged, but he continues to study magic, attempting to gather enough knowledge and understanding of magic to better face the shadow when next they meet. After his graduation, Ged embarks on many adventures, including saving a poor island town from a dragon. All along, he is pursued by the shadow, until he decides that it is his destiny to confront it. After a long journey to an island far out on the ocean, he meets the shadow face to face at last. At the same moment, Ged and the shadow speak the name "Ged," and the two combine into one entity. Having recognized his own shadow and fusing with the darkness that was in him, Ged has overcome it with his own light, and he becomes a wiser and more whole wizard.

The notion of a shadow that follows the hero was inspired by Hans Christian Andersen's "The Shadow," in which a man's shadow, through a lengthy series of events, detaches from his owner and betrays him, resulting in the man's execution. Le Guin also drew influence from the teaching of Carl Jung, the German psychiatrist who saw the shadow as a metaphor for the opposite side of a person's nature. "The shadow is the other side of our psyche, the dark brother of the conscious mind," Le Guin observed.

> The shadow stands on the threshold between the conscious and the unconscious mind, and we meet it in our dreams, as sister, brother, friend, beast, monster, enemy, guide. It is all we don't want to, can't, admit into our conscious self, all the qualities and tendencies within us which have been repressed, denied, or not used.[10]

RACE IN EARTHSEA

A Wizard of Earthsea should be noted for its being one of the first fantasy novels to feature a predominately non-white cast of characters. Many of the characters in Le Guin's books are of mixed ethnicity, and the world of the Earthsea stories is no different. When the television mini-series *Legends of Earthsea*, based on her work, aired in 2004, Le Guin expressed dismay at the choice to cast the film with mostly white actors, something that went against the entire philosophy of her book. "My protagonist is Ged, a boy with red-brown skin. In the film, he's a petulant white kid,"[11] she observed. In her essay, "A Whitewashed

Earthsea" in *Slate*, Le Guin explained her choice to make her characters an ethnicity other than white:

> My color scheme was conscious and deliberate from the start. . . . I didn't see why everybody in heroic fantasy had to be white (and why all the leading women had "violet eyes"). It didn't even make sense. Whites are a minority on Earth now—why wouldn't they still be either a minority, or just swallowed up in the larger colored gene pool, in the future?
>
> The fantasy tradition I was writing in came from Northern Europe, which is why it was about white people. I'm white, but not European. My people could be any color I liked, and I like red and brown and black. I was a little wily about my color scheme. I figured some white kids (the books were published for "young adults") might not identify straight off with a brown kid, so I kind of eased the information about skin color in by degrees—hoping that the reader would get "into Ged's skin" and only then discover it wasn't a white one. . . .
>
> I think it is possible that some readers never even notice what color the people in the story are. Don't notice, don't care. Whites of course have the privilege of not caring, of being "colorblind." Nobody else does.
>
> I have heard, not often, but very memorably, from readers of color who told me that the Earthsea books were the only books in the genre that they felt included in—and how much this meant to them, particularly as adolescents, when they'd found nothing to read in fantasy and science fiction except the adventures of white people in white worlds. Those letters have been a tremendous reward and true joy to me. . . .
>
> As an anthropologist's daughter, I am intensely conscious of the risk of cultural or ethnic imperialism—a white writer speaking for nonwhite people, co-opting their voice, an act of

extreme arrogance. In a totally invented fantasy world, or in a far-future science fiction setting, in the rainbow world we can imagine, this risk is mitigated. That's the beauty of science fiction and fantasy—freedom of invention.[12]

CRITICAL ACCLAIM

A Wizard of Earthsea was hailed upon its release and today occupies a place of honor alongside some of the greatest fantasy novels of all time. In *Death Ray*, Guy Haley remarked:

> The book is bursting with Le Guin's inventiveness. Earthsea, with its thousands of islands, resembles a temperate Indonesia, its combination of multiple cultures and seafaring traditions setting it far above other, more formulaic fantasies. . . . Le Guin writes like she is documenting reality, and nowhere is this more apparent than in her Earthsea books.[13]

FILMING EARTHSEA

Hollywood has attempted to bring Le Guin's world of Earthsea to life on the screen for a number of years. In 2004, following the great success of Peter Jackson's Academy Award–winning adaptation of Tolkien's *The Lord of the Rings*, the SciFi channel premiered *Legends of Earthsea*, a miniseries loosely based on *A Wizard of Earthsea* and its sequel *The Tombs of Atuan*. Le Guin, who was not involved at all in the movie's production, has been very vocal about her displeasure regarding how her material was handled. "The people who made it, having smarmed me with promises to respect the story and to honour the consultative capacity given me in the contract, didn't," she told *Death Ray*.

> Having hyped or lied about who was to write the screenplay, they gave it to a hack. The casting and directing were as

In 2006, Japanese director Goro Miyazaki adapted two of Ursula K.
Le Guin's Earthsea *novels into the* Gedo Senki, *or* Tales of Earthsea.
Le Guin was more pleased with this animated film adaptation than the
live-action Legends of Earthsea, *an American television miniseries*
that had been released two years earlier.

feeble and foolish as the writing. I feel sorry for a couple of the older actors. Everybody else concerned deserves nothing but derision. Including me, for letting myself be fooled by some Hollywood jerks looking for a free ride on the back of an author's name.[14]

As previously mentioned, one of Le Guin's concerns with the adaptation was the fact that the entire cast was white, despite her protagonist, Ged, being described as having red-brown skin. (Veteran actor Danny Glover is the only man of color among the main characters in the miniseries.) Le Guin called it a "far cry from the Earthsea I envisioned. When I looked over the script, I realized the producers had no understanding of what the books are about and no interest in finding out. All they intended was to use the name Earthsea . . . in a generic McMagic movie with a meaningless plot based on sex and violence."[15]

In 2006, Goro Miyazaki, the son of famed Japanese animator Hayao Miyazaki, released *Tales from Earthsea*, an animated film that loosely combines the stories of *A Wizard of Earthsea* with the plots of the third book, *The Farthest Shore*, and fourth book, *Tehanu*. Although Le Guin was far more complimentary of this adaptation, she still felt that it missed the mark. "Much of it was exciting," she wrote on her Web site.

> The excitement was maintained by violence, to a degree that I find deeply untrue to the spirit of the books. Much of it was, I thought, incoherent. This may be because I kept trying to find and follow the story of my books while watching an entirely different story, confusingly enacted by people with the same names as in my story, but with entirely different temperaments, histories, and destinies.[16]

Still, in spite of the failures to bring a fully realized, true-to-it-origins version of *Earthsea* to the screen thus far, Le Guin is hopeful that one day, Ged's adventures will unfold in movie theaters in a more honest treatment. But, she told *Death Ray*, in order for that to happen, "a filmmaker with genuine imagination . . . will have to come along. . . . Michael Powell . . . wrote a lovely little script for the first two books, years ago; but fantasy films were out of fashion then and he couldn't sell it; and then [Francis Ford] Coppola, who was backing him, went broke. Since then nobody of any stature has come along."[17]

An aerial view of a group of people atop the Ross Ice Shelf in Antarctica. An image of a pair of people pulling a sled across such an icy expanse inspired Ursula K. Le Guin to write her award-winning novel, **The Left Hand of Darkness.**

6

Gender and Race in Space

WHILE WRITING AT her desk one day, Ursula K. Le Guin was struck by an image in her mind. It was a picture of two people, she could not tell whom, pulling a sled along through a snowy, icy wasteland. The image stayed with her and, in time, blossomed into *The Left Hand of Darkness* first published in 1969.

One of Le Guin's most accomplished and revered works, *The Left Hand of Darkness* tells the story of Genly Ai, an Earth-born man of African descent, who as a representative of the Ekumen (the 80 or so worlds that form the galactic federation known as the League of All Worlds), has traveled to the planet Gethen (the word for "winter," in the language of its natives). His plan is to help the gender-neutral citizens of the Gethenian country of Karhide to join the Ekumen. The Karhide king, insane and paranoid, is resistant to Genly's invitation. At first, Estraven, Karhide's prime minister, aids Genly in his mission, but after Estraven falls from grace, the former prime minister is forced to leave the kingdom or face death.

Genly, feeling betrayed, makes for the neighboring city of Orgoreyn, where Estraven has been exiled, in hopes of successfully completing his mission. However, he is betrayed by a group that had once supported him. He is rescued by Estraven, who, as it turns out, has been the only one who supported Genly from the beginning, and the two set out to return to Karhide. The two undergo a perilous 800-mile (1,287.5-kilometers) journey across the ice-encrusted wastelands of Gethen. During this harrowing adventure, Genly and Estraven form a strong bond and come to rely on each other greatly.

Upon arriving in Karhide, Estraven is shot by enemy agents and dies, sacrificing himself so that Genly's mission can be a success. Genly is able to send a signal to the Ekumen, at which point the king of Karhide agrees to join them. The mission is a success, though a bittersweet one, as Genly feels the loss of his friend deeply.

The Left Hand of Darkness was partially inspired by Le Guin's long-standing fascination with great explorers. She had long been intrigued by the adventures of such noted explorers as Robert Falcon Scott, the British explorer who endeavored to reach the South Pole in the early twentieth century, and Ernest Shackleton, a fellow Briton who had served with Scott and went on to fame for his *Endurance* expedition, which attempted to make the first land-crossing

Did you know...

The setting and many of the adventures in Ursula K. Le Guin's *The Left Hand of Darkness* were inspired by the daring exploits of the late nineteenth and early twentieth centuries, who sought to reach the fabled South Pole.

One of the most notable of these explorers was Ernest Shackleton. A British-born officer with the Merchant Navy, Shackleton acquired his own ship, the *Nimrod,* and underwent a death-defying journey toward the South Pole. Though he did not reach the Pole itself, Shackleton made a number of scientific and geographical discoveries.

Shackleton's next great exploration was aboard the *Endurance* in a bid to make the first successful crossing of Antarctica. His plan was to send two ships, the *Endurance* and the *Aurora*, to opposite sides of the continent, with one laying supply lines to the other to ensure survival through the crossing. Unfortunately, the *Endurance* became trapped in ice in the Weddell Sea and was forced to remain there throughout the winter of 1915. Eventually, the ice crushed the ship and sank it, leaving Shackleton and his crew stranded on the ice with no means of escape. After traveling with his crew to Elephant Island, Shackleton and five others sailed to South Georgia Island for help; the remaining *Endurance* crew was rescued several months later and the men of the *Aurora* were picked up in January 1917. Shackleton attempted to return to Antarctica on one last expedition, but quietly passed away aboard the *Quest* before reaching the continent.

of the Antarctic continent. "They were certainly heroes to me, all of them," wrote Le Guin.

> And as I followed them step by frostbitten-toed step across the Ross Ice Barrier and up the Beardmore Glacier to the awful place, the white plateau, and back again, many times, they got into my toes and my bones and my books, and I wrote *The Left Hand of Darkness*, in which a Black man from Earth and an androgynous extraterrestrial pull Scott's sledge through Shackleton's blizzards across a planet called Winter.[1]

GENDER ROLES

The Left Hand of Darkness is an interesting book in Le Guin's bibliography, as it examines the roles men and women portray in society in very open and honest terms. The Gethenians are neither male nor female, and they are capable of changing genders. The reason behind this particular plot device, Le Guin writes, was an experiment. In her essay "Is Gender Necessary?" she explained:

> Because of our lifelong social conditioning it is hard for us to see clearly what, besides purely psychological form and function, truly differentiates men and women. Are there real differences in temperament, capacity, talent, psychic processes, etc.? If so, what are they? . . . I eliminated gender to find out what was left. Whatever was left would be, presumably, simply human. It would define the area that is shared by men and women alike.[2]

Today, the novel is considered the first and one of the finest examples of feminist science fiction. Le Guin also found great commercial and critical success with *The Left Hand of Darkness*. The novel won a Nebula Award in 1969 for Best Novel and a Hugo Award in 1970 for Best Novel.

*During the Imperial Trans-Antarctic Expedition, Ernest Shackleton's
ship,* Endurance, *was crushed by ice and sank, stranding her 28-man
complement on the ice. What Shackleton and his men did to survive
in the Antarctic inspired many of the experiences Ursula K. Le Guin's
characters endured in* The Left Hand of Darkness.

Did you know...

The Hugo Awards

The Hugo, named for *Amazing Stories* founder Hugo Gernsback, is an award given annually to the best science fiction and fantasy writing released in the past year. The awards were first presented in 1953, though they did not become a yearly event until 1955. Notable winners of the Hugo Award for best novel include *Ender's Game* by Orson Scott Card, *Green Mars* by Kim Stanley Robinson, and *Coraline* by Neil Gaiman. Hugos are also given to movies in the Best Dramatic Presentation category. Among the movies that won Hugos are *Star Wars, Back to the Future, The Lord of the Rings: The Fellowship of the Ring*, and *WALL-E*.

The Nebula Awards

The Nebula is presented each year by the Science Fiction and Fantasy Writers of America for outstanding works in the sci-fi and fantasy genre. The awards had their origin when a man named Lloyd Biggle Jr., who was secretary-treasurer of the SFFWA, suggested that the association (then called the Science Fiction Writers of America) put out a collection of the year's best stories. The idea soon grew into a full-blown awards ceremony. The first awards were given in 1965 and included among the winners Frank Herbert's groundbreaking novel *Dune*. Other notable winners include *Flowers For Algernon* by Daniel Keyes, *Rendezvous with Rama* by Arthur C. Clarke, and *Neuromancer* by William Gibson. As with the Hugo Awards, science fiction films are also eligible for Nebulas. Past winners include *WALL-E, Serenity, Pan's Labyrinth*, and *Galaxy Quest*.

Following the success of *The Left Hand of Darkness*, Le Guin decided to retreat from the far-off worlds of Hain and Earthsea and travel not to an imagined realm, but to her hometown of Portland, Oregon, and into the depths of the human mind and the landscape of our dreams.

Seen above, the skyline of Portland, Oregon, with Mount Hood in the background. In the novel The Lathe of Heaven, *Ursula K. Le Guin's main character has dreams that help to reshape reality. In one such dream, Mount Hood becomes an active volcano again.*

7

From Portland to Dreamland

LE GUIN'S NEXT NOVEL, *The Lathe of Heaven* (1971), was a departure from the incredible science fiction and fantasy of her Hainish and Earthsea works, taking place in Portland, Oregon, in the comparatively near future of 2002 and being much more grounded in a realistic setting. Writing in the early 1970s, Le Guin proves to be rather prophetic, as the world of the early twenty-first century that she imagines is not unlike the world in which we live today: The economy is collapsing, famine and global warming are threatening the planet, and the United States is at war with the Middle East.

In choosing to break from her usual realms and explore a near-future setting, Le Guin wrote:

> Along in 1967–68 I finally got my pure fantasy vein separated off from my science fiction vein by writing *A Wizard of Earthsea* and then *The Left Hand of Darkness*, and the separation marked a very large advance in both skill and content. Since then I have gone on writing, as it were, with both the left and the right hands; and it has been a matter of keeping on pushing out towards the limits—my own and those of the medium.[1]

The novel tells the story of George Orr, an ordinary man whose dreams have the power to alter reality. If there is something he wants in life and he dreams about it, the entire world changes around him so that he may have it.

When Portland is destroyed by a nuclear blast, Orr dreams the explosion away, which not only saves his life, but also everyone else in his city and in the United States as well. Despite having used his unusual gift to save the world, Orr feels that the power he wields is too much for one man and seeks to suppress it with various drugs. It is at this point that Dr. William Haber, a psychiatrist Orr is seeing in this new reality, enters the story.

Haber is a creation of Orr's, willed into reality in the aftermath of the nuclear explosion. Because stopping that event sapped so much of his strength, Orr was unable to create a psychiatrist sympathetic to his needs. As a result, Haber is ambitious, self-serving, and bent on using Orr's gifts to improve the world around him. Unfortunately, his plans backfire. For example, he hypnotizes Orr into dreaming of a less overpopulated world, which results in Orr creating a cancer plague that wipes out billions of people.

Eventually, Dr. Haber is able to harness the power of George Orr's dreams and use them to improve his status.

Using a machine called the Augmentor, Haber enhances Orr's abilities and bends them to his own ends. Haber makes himself head of a dream research institute and sees his wealth and status increase. When Haber demands that Orr dream of world peace, Orr conjures up an alien invasion that forces all the nations of the world to unite. When Orr attempts to undo this dream, he creates a new reality in which the aliens now live on Earth and are being bombed by the United States Air Force. This results in Mount Hood, a dormant volcano that overlooks Portland, becoming active again.

During this time, Orr has become romantically involved with Heather LeLache, a black lawyer whom he has consulted in hopes of freeing himself from Haber's treatments. Unfortunately, when Haber forces Orr to dream of a world without racism, George creates a world in which everyone's skin color is gray. In this new world, he and Heather are separated.

As Haber's power grows, he becomes the ruler of Portland, which is now the capital city of the world. His lust to rule grows to be all-consuming, so much so that he attempts to use the Augmentor in an effort to harness Orr's power for himself. This creates a new reality, one that is at odds with Orr's established reality, and the very fabric of the universe begins to unravel. Using his sheer will, Orr is able to reach the Augmentor and shut it off, resulting in Haber's mind being left irreparably shattered. Orr, however, is free. He takes a new job working for an alien, and he meets Heather again, though her memories of him are gone.

CRITICS RAVE

Upon its release, *The Lathe of Heaven* was very well received by critics and audiences alike. The noted sci-fi author Philip K. Dick complimented Le Guin's novel in his essay "Man, Android and Machine":

> One of the best novels, and most important to understanding of the nature of our world, is Ursula Le Guin's *The Lathe of*

Did you know...

In 1984, a small town located near Le Guin's hometown of Portland, Oregon, held a hearing to debate whether or not *The Lathe of Heaven* was suitable for a senior high school literature class. Some who opposed the book deemed it immoral and filled with anti-Christian sentiments. According to Le Guin, they also classified the book as the equivalent of "junk food." Many people in the school district, however, spoke out in favor of the book, including many of the school's students themselves, and the motion to ban it was defeated.

After the vote, Le Guin published an essay on the topic in *The Oregonian*, in which she used the incident as a means of illustrating how wrong it is to censor books. "Censorship, here or in Russia or wherever, is absolutely anti-democratic and elitist," she wrote. "The censor says: You don't know enough to choose, but we do, so you will read what we choose for you and nothing else. The democrat says: The process of learning is that of learning how to choose. Freedom isn't given, it's earned. Read, learn, and earn it."[*]

[*]Barbara J. Bucknall, *Ursula K. Le Guin*. New York: Fredrick Ungar Publishing Co., 1981, p. 19.

Heaven, in which the dream universe is articulated in such a striking and compelling way that I hesitate to add any further explanation to it; it requires none.[2]

Receiving such a compliment from Dick was particularly meaningful to Le Guin, as the author served as something of an inspiration when writing the book. "You could almost call it 'Homage à Dick,'" she said in an interview with Larry McCaffery and Sinda Gregory. "My approach was like saying, 'This is one great way to write a novel, invented by Philip K. Dick.' That's one thing about science fiction: writers in the genres are less uptight about imitation and emulation than 'mainstream' people. Writing should be really more like music, with its healthy spirit of borrowing."[3]

DREAMS AND PHILOSOPHIES

The Lathe of Heaven was partially inspired by Le Guin's interest in the dream research of the 1960s, as well as her overall interest in the subject of dreaming. "I was fascinated with that," she said.

> The scientists that were writing it mostly wrote very well, but actually they didn't get very far. There has been no breakthrough since the seventies in sleep and dream research, or not much. But it seemed like they were going to be able to explain what dreaming is and what it does. And that's the period when I picked up the idea for *The Lathe of Heaven*, which is simply "what if dreams came true," and take it literally, take a metaphor.[4]

Another major source of influence in *The Lathe of Heaven* was Le Guin's interest in Taoism, the ancient Chinese philosophy, and the *Tao Te Ching*, a text written by Lao Tzu that has influenced much of Chinese religious thought over the past several centuries. The title itself is a reference to a passage from the writings of the Taoist

Lao Tzu (above), an ancient Chinese philosopher, is considered to be the founder of Taoism. This philosophical and religious tradition began in ancient China and has influenced countless people, including Le Guin. The title of her novel, The Lathe of Heaven, *is a quote taken from the writings of Chuang Tse, a central figure in Taoism.*

philosopher Chuang Tse, which says: "Those whom heaven helps we call the sons of heaven. They do not learn this by learning. They do not work it by working. They do not reason it by using reason. To let understanding stop at what cannot be understood is a high attainment. Those who cannot do it will be destroyed on the lathe of heaven."[5]

As a child, Le Guin was first introduced to the *Tao Te Ching* via a translation of the work that sat on her father's bookshelf. "He clearly got a great lifelong pleasure out of this book, and when you notice a parent doing something like this, it's bound to have some effect on you. So when I was twelve years old I had a look at the thing and . . . I loved it. By the time I was in my teens I had thought about it quite a lot."[6]

In the novel, the characters reflect the teachings of Taoism in their words and actions, and each chapter begins with quotes from either Lao Tzu or Chuang Tse. "*The Lathe of Heaven* is a Taoist novel," Le Guin said, "not a utopian or dystopian one. . . . Haber is a utopian, yes: and he tries to use George's dreams to achieve his quite rational notions of how things might be improved: but every time he tries it, things get worse. There is an old American saying, 'If it ain't broke, don't fix it.' The novel extends that a bit—'Even if it's broke, if you don't know how to fix it, don't.'"[7]

THE LATHE ON FILM

Unlike Le Guin's other works, most of which have not been adapted for film, *The Lathe of Heaven* was the subject of not one, but two film versions. The first aired on PBS in 1980 and starred Bruce Davison as George Orr. Le Guin has commented very favorably on this adaptation, despite its being made for a modest budget of $250,000. In fact, the budget for the 1980 adaptation was so small that the alien spacecrafts featured in the movie were actually Frisbees!

Le Guin recounts her experiences working on the film in her essay "Working on *The Lathe*," in which she describes the various details of the production and her experiences as a moviemaking novice. At the conclusion of production, Le Guin sat in on the recording sessions for the musical score for the film and realized how it summarized her overall experiences. "This rawboned beast of a movie we have worked on so long is transformed, transfigured, by the music; the music for this scene, this moment; the music of this work," she wrote. "It comes together, now, at last. All the months; all the money; all the machinery; all the many people. It comes together. We have made it."[8]

Of the film itself, Le Guin is very complimentary, though she acknowledges that its small budget limited the movie somewhat. "Well, we sure could have used another quarter of a million bucks, but I think we turned a shoestring into a pretty good silk purse," she said.

> Since the tight budget forced us to shoot in a few weeks, without retakes, in Dallas not Portland, we couldn't get the close, gritty, local texture of life I longed for. . . . But not only is the film faithful to the sense of the book; the acting, the directing, the camera work, the music, all of very high quality, integrate and work together to make a strong, vivid film, quite independent of the book. Yes, I like it.[9]

In 2002, the novel was made into a movie a second time, this time for the A&E Network. Starring James Caan as Haber, Lukas Haas as George Orr, and Lisa Bonet as Heather LaLache, this adaptation, simply titled *Lathe of Heaven*, was not as well received. In *Variety*, critic Michael Speier derided the remake: "Ursula Le Guin's 1971 sci-fi vision of a lobotomized future and, specifically, one man's therapy gone awry is still provocative on the surface—what could happen if someone controlled our dreams?—but the execution here ranges from low-key to lackluster to downright boring."[10]

THE WORD FOR WORLD IS FOREST

In 1972, Le Guin followed up the success of *The Lathe of Heaven* by penning a novella, *The Word for World Is*

Forest. A return to her Hainish cycle of stories, the novella concerns travelers from Earth who arrive on a planet known as Athshe (a word that means "forest" in the language of the natives). The native inhabitants are three-foot-tall (0.9-m-tall) humanoids whose bodies are covered in green fur. The humans have been logging and deforesting the planet for several years, due to the fact that Earth is now almost entirely covered by concrete and urban development. As a result, wood is now considered to be the most precious commodity in the universe. Their deforestation efforts have come with the promise that the land will be re-tilled by farmers, but so much of the plant and tree life has been destroyed that Athshe is slowly becoming a desert.

The people of Athshe are easily conquered by the invading humans, who take advantage of their docile temperaments and the fact that they never seem to sleep. The Athsheans are quickly enslaved and treated cruelly by their captors. One of the worst offenders is a man named Captain Don Davidson. Le Guin writes him as a cliché of the strong-jawed patriotic heroes who dominated the science-fiction tales she read as a child. Unlike those virtuous heroes of old, Davidson is a sadist who abuses the Athsheans mercilessly, calling them "creechies" (short for "creatures"). Le Guin has since described this character as one she did not like writing as much. "He was a pretty terrifying voice for me to write because he's a highly aggressive, sadistic man," she said. "But then, he is part of me, obviously. I wrote him and accept him as part of myself."[11] When his violent behavior results in the death of the wife of an Athshean named Selver, Davidson soon finds himself battling an army of angry natives intent on reclaiming their planet.

The Word for World Is Forest was first published in the novella collection *Again, Dangerous Visions* in 1972, edited by Harlan Ellison. The story was inspired by Le Guin's reaction to the Vietnam War, which lasted from 1959 until 1975 and divided the American people, many of whom felt the United States' involvement in the war was wrong. She recalled:

> I was living in London when I wrote that novel. I couldn't march so I wrote. I prefer, though, to keep my activism out of my art; if I can march downtown with a banner, it seems a lot more direct than blithering about it in a novel. When I was in London I couldn't do anything and I had an anger building up inside me, which came out when I was writing that novel. It may have hurt that book from an artistic standpoint.[12]

One aspect of the Athsheans that is a large part of the novel is their ability to create vivid dreams that, to them, are indiscernible from reality. This notion was inspired by an anthropological study of the Senoi people of Malaysia, who, according to the studies of Dr. Charles Tart, used dreams to influence their daily lives. They would discuss their dreams, analyze them, and use them to improve the world around them. According to this study, Le Guin wrote:

> The Senoi dream is meaningful, active and creative. Adults deliberately go into their dreams to solve problems of inter-personal and intercultural conflict. They come out of their dreams with a new song, tool, dance, idea. The waking and the dreaming states are equally valid, each acting upon the other in complementary fashion. . . . It appears that the Senoi have not had a war, or a murder, for several hundred years.[13]

Much of the study has since been disproved, but Le Guin found it to be a concept interesting enough to incorporate into the book. "It was very exciting when it was first published," she said later,

> and it seemed to be good scientific evidence for people actually using dreams as a community enterprise. And apparently the [Senoi] people do encourage people to tell their dreams. They tell each other dreams and if it's an important dream they discuss it. . . . I thought that was endearing, and interesting, and so I played with it in that book.[14]

Le Guin later expanded on the themes of the novella in a full-fledged novel edition of *The Word for World Is Forest*, which was published in 1976.

RETURN TO EARTHSEA

In 1971, Le Guin returned to the world of Earthsea with *The Tombs of Atuan*, the second book in the Earthsea series, which was inspired by the author's traveling through the high desert of her home state of Oregon. "In 1969, my husband and I spent a couple nights in French Glen, the mountainous area of southeastern Oregon," she said.

> It was my first sight of that sagebrush high-desert terrain, and it got into me so instantly and authoritatively that a book grew out of it—*The Tombs of Atuan*. The book isn't about the desert but about a community surrounded by a terrain similar to what you find in southeastern Oregon. The desert is a buried metaphor in the book. I have no idea of the reason for the emotional economy of it, but I know the book came to me as I was driving back from French Glen.[15]

The protagonist of *The Tombs of Atuan* is a priestess named Tenar who lives in the Kargad Empire on the island of Atuan. The people of Atuan, more religious in nature, do not believe in magic and possess a hatred for wizards and wizardry. Tenar lives a solitary existence on her island, spending much of her time in quiet contemplation in the dark tombs of the book's title; they create the temple of the Nameless Ones, the dark powers worshipped by her people.

When she is 15, Tenar meets Ged, the hero of *A Wizard of Earthsea*. Ged has come to Atuan in search of the ring of Erreth-Akbe, a sacred talisman that has been broken in half. Ged has one half but needs to unite the ring in order to bring peace to Earthsea. Tenar, who had been renamed Arha by those who follow the dark religion of the Nameless Ones, is given back her true name by Ged and leads him to the other half of the ring. Using his magic, he is able to unite the ring and the two escape Atuan, leaving the tombs to crumble in an earthquake. The two travel to Havnor, the largest island of Earthsea's archipelago and the capital of the Kings of Earthsea. There, Tenar wishes to remain with Ged, but he tells her that he must leave her, for he has other matters to attend to.

By leaving Tenar on Havnor, Ged has given her independence and freedom, something she had not had on Atuan. In becoming independent rather than falling into the arms of the hero and becoming his wife, Tenar becomes a female character of some empowerment. This choice was a very conscious one for Le Guin. "*The Tombs of Atuan* was the first book I wrote, I think, the first real full scale, large size novel with a woman at the center," she said.

> But of course it becomes a pair. It becomes a man and a woman when Ged comes into the book, although we are always in Tenar's mind, she is the viewpoint character always, that's very important who is seeing the working. Ged is important because they have to act together to make anything happen.[16]

Le Guin followed *The Tombs of Atuan* with *The Farthest Shore*, the third book of Earthsea, published in 1972. In it, a breach in the world of Earthsea is causing magic to lose its power. In an effort to seal the breach, Ged and a young prince must make a perilous journey to the land of the dead. "*The Farthest Shore* is about death," Le Guin observed. "That's why it is a less well built, less sound and complete book than the others. They were about things I had already lived through and survived. *The Farthest Shore* is about the thing you do not live through and survive."[17]

Despite the book's rather heavy subject matter, Le Guin has said that she feels it is well suited to younger readers, since, she explained, "in a way one can say that the hour when a child realizes, not that death exists—children are intensely aware of death—but that he/she, personally, is mortal, will die, is the hour when childhood ends, and the new life begins. Coming of age again, but in a larger context."[18] *The Farthest Shore* was well received, earning the National Book Award for 1972.

Before her next novel, *The Dispossessed*, was published, Le Guin warned readers that it was a book that pushed her style beyond the limits of what they had come to expect from her so far. "I hope rending sounds and cries of dismay are not heard when it comes out,"[19] she wrote. As time would soon tell, she need not have worried.

Ursula K. Le Guin at home in Portland, Oregon, in December 2005. In the late 1970s, Le Guin began to move away from fantasy and science fiction and into other genres, including young adult fiction.

8

Anarchy in Space

RELEASED IN 1974, *The Dispossessed* (subtitled *An Ambiguous Utopia*) proved to be among Ursula K. Le Guin's most successful and well-received novels, garnering both the Hugo and Nebula awards. Oddly enough, this successful novel had its origins in a short story that the author disliked intensely. "*The Dispossessed* came with a perfectly awful short story, one of the worst things I ever wrote," Le Guin later said.

> There it was, all about prison camps, everything in it all backwards, a monstrosity of a little story. Then I thought, "You know, it's really terrible that you could write anything that bad after writing all these years; there's got to be something in it." . . . That one

took real homework. But sure enough, the idea had been there all along; I just hadn't understood it.[1]

The Dispossessed takes place on Anarres and Urras, twin inhabited worlds. Urras is a capitalistic world, with a governmental structure similar to that of the United States, while Anarres is an anarchist society without an organized system of government. The book begins approximately 200 years after an anarchist faction broke away from Urras and was granted permission to set up a colony on Anarres. Because the colonists living on Anarres have had little contact with Urras, a sense of distrust and fear toward their former home exists in the colony. Meanwhile, Urras depends on Anarres to supply them with badly needed metals, as they had exhausted their own supplies many years before.

The main character of the novel is a physicist named Shevek, who has lived his entire life on Anarres. His research regarding theories of time leads him to a belief that the political structure of his world is not the utopian society he had once believed it to be. Therefore, Shevek decides to embark on a journey to Urras to both learn from its society and to bring its citizens the knowledge and history from his. During his travels, Shevek comes to realize that no society is perfect. Entranced at first by the wealth and splendor of Urras, specifically its capitalist nation of A-Io, he soon sees the planet's other side, where the poor live in squalor without access to decent health care. As the book progresses, he returns to Anarres, hoping to help bridge the gap between the two societies.

The Dispossessed has been hailed as much for its sharp political commentary as it has for its storytelling. Many critics have seen the book as an interesting study on the

Did you know...

While the term "anarchy" has come to symbolize chaos, lawlessness, and a world without order, the philosophy actually advocates a society in which the state or governing body does not control society; instead, everyone works together for the betterment of the civilization as a whole.

Certain incidents, however, served to sour the public's opinion of anarchism. One of the most notorious was the 1886 Haymarket Bombing in Chicago, in which a bomb killed a police officer. Following the bombing, eight prominent anarchists were arrested and charged with murder. Despite the fact that there was no evidence connecting them with the bombing, the prosecution used their speeches and writings against the defendants and all eight were convicted, with seven being sentenced to death.

Regardless of anarchism's negative perception, Le Guin still believes that the tenets of the philosophy are sound:

> We have followed the state far enough—too far, in fact. The state is leading us to World War Three. The whole idea of the state has got to be rethought from the beginning and then dismantled. One way to do this is to propose the most extreme solution imaginable: you don't proceed little by little, you go to the extreme and say let's have no government, no state at all. Then you try to figure out what you have without it, which is essentially what I was trying to do in *The Dispossessed*.*

*Carl Freedman, ed., *Conversations with Ursula K. Le Guin*, Jackson, Miss.: University Press of Mississippi, 2008, p. 42.

This color wood engraving depicts the Haymarket Affair that took place on May 4, 1886, in Chicago, Illinois. The bomb that exploded in the crowd was blamed on anarchists. The anarchist philosophy helps to inform the governmental structure of one of the twin planets Ursula K. Le Guin explores in her award-winning novel **The Dispossessed.**

nature of both anarchism and capitalism. Le Guin herself has said that she based the society of Anarres on the anarchist societies that flourished in Spain during the late 1930s before Francisco Franco took power and eliminated the anarchists by force.

The Dispossessed was also praised for its structure. The odd-numbered chapters are set on Urras, while the even-numbered chapters take place on Annares. The book is notable also for its leaps back and forth in time throughout the narrative, which shows the reader Shevek's childhood and how his past experiences led him to the places we find him in throughout the novel.

BACK TO EARTH

Following The Dispossessed, Le Guin veered from science fiction and published Very Far Away from Anywhere Else, a short book for young readers first published in 1976. The story concerns a young man named Owen Griffiths, who has an aptitude for science, and his friendship with Natalie Field, a talented young musician. Owen and Natalie come to trust and confide in each other amidst the terrible peer pressure that exists in high school. As they grow to be closer, Owen confides in Natalie about Thorn, the fantasy world he has created in his mind. Rather than making fun of him, she shows great interest and offers to compose music for this imaginary country. A touching, coming-of-age story, Very Far Away from Anywhere Else was later named an American Library Association Notable Book for Young Adults.

Le Guin's next novel, The Eye of the Heron (1978), represented a bold leap forward for the author, as it turned out to be what she considers to be her first consciously feminist work. Initially the hero of the book was a young man named Lev, but as Le Guin soon learned while writing, it was not to be Lev's story after all. "The young man insisted upon getting killed," she said. "And I said, 'Please, don't do that, you're my hero, don't please Lev, don't die.' 'Stop,' he says.

'I'm off, good bye!' And it became a story about a young woman because she had to take over. . . . And after that, then I began to sort of comfortably be a woman, and my writing changed a good deal."[2]

As the 1970s drew to a close, Le Guin also published two books that took place in Orsinia, the fictional country she had created almost two decades earlier. The first book, *Orsinian Tales*, published in 1976, was a collection of short stories that cover the history of Orsinia from the Middle Ages through the cultural and political upheaval of the 1960s. The second book, *Malafrena*, takes place over the course of five years, beginning in 1825, and deals with a young aristocrat who leaves his father's estate (located in a valley called Malafrena) to take part in a revolution happening in the capital.

Le Guin had been working on *Malafrena* since she was in her twenties, but getting into the right mindset to finish it properly took some time. "I can't say *Malafrena* was like one of those books found in the bottom of a trunk," Le Guin said; "it kept coming out of the trunk and being worked on, and then hurled back in despair. Until I finally grew up enough to write it."[3]

In her novel Always Coming Home, *Ursula K. Le Guin explored the Napa Valley region in California. Her family has long-standing ties to the region, where she spent every summer of her childhood and many important parts of her adult life.*

9

The Worlds Beyond

COMING INTO A NEW decade, Ursula K. Le Guin was no less productive than she had been in the past. In 1980, she published *The Beginning Place*, a short novel that deals with two youths from troubled backgrounds who stumble across a hidden place, Tembreabrezi, where time flows more slowly than in the real world. She followed this book with an ambitious novel, *Always Coming Home*. Released in 1985, the novel told the story of the Kesh, a group of people who live many years from now in the Napa Valley region of Northern California. The book functions partially as a straightforward narrative—telling the tale of Stone Telling, a Kesh woman at odds with the rigid ways of her people—but it also works as an anthropological text by describing the culture and history of the Kesh people through poems, songs, legends, and even recipes.

The idea for the novel came from Le Guin's desire to write about people living in a walled city somewhere in the Andes Mountains of South America. As she began to delve deeper into the concept, she had something of a revelation regarding the setting for the story. "I realized that what I wanted to write about was literally my home, the property in the Napa Valley in California, which is still in my family, where I spent every summer of my childhood and have been almost every year of my life even if only for a brief moment," she explained. "And this piece of land which is extremely dear to me, I wanted to write a story about the people living there who were worthy of living there, who were using that very beautiful country properly instead of what's happened to the Napa Valley now."[1]

In preparing to write the book, Le Guin traveled back to Napa and spent the entire spring of 1982 living there, working and researching the region. "I didn't know how many kinds of oak grew in California," she said. "I had to make a considerable study and indeed I took notes. It's a small example of the kind of research or reading that I did for that book. Educating myself to the flora and fauna and climate and geology of California, because I wanted to get it right."[2]

Writing *Always Coming Home* presented some interesting new challenges for Le Guin. For starters, she found herself having to invent an entire language. "When I conceived the book," she said, "I thought of Kesh as being a non-existent language from which I was going to translate, which was a lot of fun. But finally, after most of the book had been written, it had to become at least a partly existing language from which I could translate, because I needed the language itself for the songs. So it led me a little deeper into language invention."[3]

In addition to creating a new language while writing *Always Coming Home*, Le Guin also discovered a talent she never knew she had: songwriting. While creating the various songs and poems for the book, Le Guin began to toy with the idea of setting them to music. She then contacted Todd Barton, a musician and composer with whom she had worked before on a radio play. "Todd can compose in any style, so I said: 'Todd, would you be interested in inventing a music for a non-existent people?'" she recalled. "And— 'Yes, yes,' he said. So then, he and I had to work together. He would send me little tapes with little sketches, compositions on them, and he would say, 'Does that sound like the Kesh to you?' and I would say, 'Well, no, no, this is too aggressive, or too Chinese,' or something."[4] The result of Le Guin and Barton's collaboration was *Music and Poetry of the Kesh*, an album of 10 musical pieces and three poems based on Le Guin's fictional characters.

In addition to the album, the book was also packaged with various detailed illustrations of the Kesh and their world, making *Always Coming Home* something of an interactive multimedia experience. "It seemed to me as if I was trying to give this sense that the reader is in this valley, among these people," Le Guin said, "and can move around in the book freely, he does not have to read the book in order, but move around and find anything that's interesting, almost like walking around in a house, that there ought to be visual and sound input as well as just the words on a page."[5]

CATWINGS TAKE FLIGHT

Le Guin closed out the 1980s by venturing into yet another uncharted region of publishing: children's books. *Catwings*, published in 1988, tells the story of four kittens who were inexplicably born with wings. Their mother, Ms. Jane Tabby, is not bothered by this, and sees their wings as a means for them to fly from their dreary city life to a more beautiful home in the country.

Unlike some of her other works, which came from grand ideas or a desire to tackle large themes, *Catwings* had a very simple, almost accidental, origin. "I drew a picture of a cat with wings, and I thought, 'Oh, what fun! Why shouldn't a cat have wings?'" said Le Guin, "and then, 'What would happen if they did?' and so there goes the book."[6]

As is typical of Le Guin, she opted not to simply tell a cute story, but rather inject her book with realism and

---

Did you know...

Because the experience of creating such a varied project in *Always Coming Home* was such a positive one, Ursula K. Le Guin entertained the notion of creating an online or CD-ROM companion for the novel. However, that idea has yet to come to fruition. "It would make a lovely CD-ROM," she noted. "There is a problem, however, with the visuals. If you noticed, in the book there are no faces."*

*Carl Freedman, ed., *Conversations with Ursula K. Le Guin*, Jackson, Miss.: University Press of Mississippi, 2008, p. 152.

address some of the plights the cats might face in the wild, such as dangerous barn owls. She also is very honest about the kittens' mother's treatment of her children in sending them away, an idea that provoked a response both from her editor and her readers. "Oh, in *Catwings*, where the narrator says something like 'that's what cat families do,' when the mother sends her kittens away, I didn't originally have that in there," Le Guin said.

> That was my wonderful editor, Dick Jackson. . . . And he said that kids will be horrified, that I was frightening children. And I thought, "I don't want to do that. But it is what cats do." And he said just to say that. So I did. I get letters from inner city kids who say, "I hate Mrs. Jane. She sent her kids away." They're very human cats. The kids identify with the kittens. There was a real flaw there that Dick caught and patched up as well as he could, but it remains an ethical catch in the book.[7]

Catwings proved to be another well-received effort from Le Guin. Writing about both *Catwings* and its sequel, *Catwings Return*, in the *Magazine of Fantasy and Science Fiction*, Orson Scott Card observed that

> even though Le Guin's stories are not sentimentalized, neither do they shock or brutalize in their truthfulness. Rather, as she makes danger and loss and injury and fear and all the passages of life seem natural and unavoidable, Le Guin also lets us see that life can still be well-lived, and individuals can still act rightly and lovingly and bravely, and can bear with dignity whatever losses come. Not a bad set of truths for children to learn in a couple of gentle, well-told tales.[8]

In addition to warm notices from her peers, Le Guin has said that the Catwings books have generated positive responses from young readers, many of whom send her their own Catwings stories. "Jane is the favorite of the kids that write me," she said. "It's very interesting. When they write their own stories, they tend to feature Jane. Though the boys write about the boy cats and they have gun battles . . . they fly airplanes. They're wonderful."[9]

Catwings spawned three sequels, *Catwings Return* (1989), *Wonderful Alexander and the Catwings* (1994), and *Jane on Her Own* (1999). Despite fans' desire for further stories, Le Guin is unsure of whether or not the Catwings characters will take flight again. "I don't know if there is going to be any more *Catwings*," she said. "My bet would be a little against."[10]

Following her success in the world of children's publishing, Le Guin decided to begin the next decade by returning to a world she thought she had left behind forever.

Although highly regarded for her fantasy and science fiction, Ursula K. Le Guin has also often written about ordinary people. In 1991, she published Searoad, *a collection of stories that take place in a fictional town on the rugged Oregon coast.*

10

Farewell to Earthsea

SUBTITLED *THE FINAL BOOK of Earthsea, Tehanu*, published in 1990, continued the story of Tenar, the female protagonist from *The Tombs of Atuan*. Now widowed and with two grown children, she lives alone on the island of Gont. After she rescues a child named Therru from her abusive father, Tenar sets out on a journey that reunites her with Ged, the hero of the previous three novels. Ged, having lost his powers of magic in the previous book, is something of a broken man. Nevertheless, his reunion with Tenar is a happy one, and they are soon married. However, dark forces are in search of Therru, and Ged and Tenar soon find themselves in a battle to protect this young girl, who appears to possess powers of her own. "I was very happy to give Tenar, whose marriage had not been very happy, and Ged . . . a joyful and powerful relationship of love," she said. "My secret name for the book while I was writing it was, 'Better Late than Never'!"[1]

Tehanu is a departure from the previous Earthsea books, in that it presents a darker and more complex story. It also differs from the novels that preceded it in that Ged, the main character, has been robbed of his powers and has been left an ordinary mortal. Further, the scope of the book is much more female-driven than previous books, something that Le Guin found challenging. She said:

> I had to learn to write as a woman, without putting men at the center of the story. The feminist movement of the sixties and seventies was a huge help to me. . . . After I had learned enough, I could come back to Earthsea, and without changing anything in it, I could see it entirely differently, because I was looking at it from a different point of view—not from the place of power, now, but from below, from the position of an "ordinary" woman and a little girl who has been terribly hurt—from the position of the powerless. From there, everything looks different![2]

In an interview with *Vice*, Le Guin recalled how these character changes and gender shifts did not sit well with some readers. "The most negative feedback related to gender I ever got was to *Tehanu*, the fourth book of Earthsea, which shifted the point of view from men of power in a male-dominated world to powerless men and women in the same world," she said. "That really irked the boys. They saw it as a betrayal. I see it as exactly the opposite."[3] Despite such criticisms, *Tehanu* was another success for the author, winning the Nebula Award for Best Novel in 1990.

Unlike the first three books, Le Guin considered *Tehanu* to be a book for a slightly older readership. "[The book] has a young child in it, but the child's been abused. And the actual protagonist is an old woman," she explained. "So it's not a book for nine-year-olds. It's a book for some twelve-year-olds these days, though. Those kids are reading amazingly sophisticated things."[4]

AN EARTHLY SHORE

Following *Tehanu*, Le Guin scaled back her visions of other worlds and far-off planets to center on a place that was close to her heart: the rugged landscape of the Oregon coast. *Searoad*, published in 1991, was a collection of short stories about the fictional Oregon town of Klatsand. "*Searoad* was a response to becoming a part-time citizen of a small Oregon coastal town," Le Guin said. "Klatsand is a composite/extract of several towns on the north Oregon coast. The book is exploration, satire and homage."[5]

Many people found it interesting that Le Guin, an author known for science fiction and fantasy, would produce a quiet, meditative book set in present-day Oregon. But for Le Guin, it was just another story she felt compelled to tell. Besides, she argued, "Oregon is a pretty exotic place to a lot of Easterners. . . . I've always written realism as well as non-realism. But if you write [science-fiction] you tend to get type-cast."[6]

The various stories in that collection chronicle the ups and downs, successes and failures, of several generations of women in Klatsand. Despite the book's relatively short length, Le Guin found that tapping into the voices of the characters was trickier than she had originally imagined. "The voices came seemingly arbitrarily in time," she said.

> They were related by the place, but they were free in time. I wish I could tell you why it was written that way. It is almost entirely in the order that it was written. It took two years to write and it's only sixty pages long. That doesn't mean I was at my desk every morning of the two years, but I was working on it in my head all the time. I had to wait for the voices to come. A voice would come and I would write down what it said, as it were, channeling again. If I tried to push it or force it or demand something to write, it would be wrong, and I'd have to throw it out. I had to sit and listen.[7]

Since most of the lead characters in *Searoad* were women, Le Guin found herself battling some critics for the book's perceived sexism. "I had to fight my own publisher from saying it was a book about women for women, and only women could possibly be interested in it," she recalled. "I said, 'My God, my sales are generally pretty good. Shall we not try to cut them in half by saying stay away from this book, boys, you'll hate it?'"[8]

Nevertheless, Le Guin found that she had to field some disapproval for *Searoad*, a task that she found somewhat difficult, as well as hard to fully understand. "Some of the criticism that has annoyed me, that hurt me, has been related to *Searoad*," she said. "Some critic said that 'all the men in the book are either weak or wicked,' which totally floored me. Kim Stanley Robinson is on me about what he calls the absence of the 'good young man.' Well, there aren't any 'good young women' in *Moby Dick*, but it's still a good book."[9]

Searoad was followed in 1994 by another short story collection, *A Fisherman of the Inland Sea*. The next year, she published a collection of Hainish stories entitled *Four Ways to Forgiveness*, followed quickly by another compilation of stories, *Unlocking the Air and Other Stories*.

RETURN OF THE EKUMEN

In 2000, she made her first full-length Hainish novel in 24 years, *The Telling*. The novel is set on the planet Aka, a world now fully consumed by technology. When Sutty, an Ekumen envoy, learns of an indigenous people living in the wild that still hold to the old ways of Aka, she travels to Aka to make a pilgrimage with them. Along her journey, she learns their ancient traditions and comes to understand their long-held belief in the Telling, the cornerstone of their religious beliefs.

The Telling was inspired by Le Guin's discovery of how Mao Tse-tung, China's autocratic leader from 1949 until his death in 1976, had all but eradicated the Taoist religion from Chinese culture during his Cultural Revolution, which lasted from 1966 until his death. Although she had been a student of the philosophy of Taoism for much of her life, Le Guin had not realized how the religion had been so terribly suppressed in China. "In one generation, one psychopathic tyrant destroyed a tradition two thousand years old," she said. "In my lifetime. And I knew nothing about it. The enormity of the event, and the enormity of my ignorance, left me stunned. I had to think about it. Since the way I think is fiction, eventually I had to write a story about it."[10]

Although many readers trumpeted *The Telling* as a long-awaited return to the Ekumen universe, Le Guin reminded them that she had been turning out Hainish stories for years, though in the form of short stories and novellas. "I thought 'The Telling' was going to be a novella too," she said, "but it insisted on being a novel. Its most obvious sources of inspiration (if that's the word) are the Cultural Revolution in China, and the rise of fundamentalist religiosity around the world in the last few decades."[11]

RETURN TO EARTHSEA

The Telling was followed quickly by a return to another universe readers thought Le Guin had left behind: Earthsea. Although *Tehanu* was famously subtitled *The Last Book of Earthsea*, it turned out that Le Guin still had more tales to tell. "I was wrong! I was wrong!" she jokingly stated regarding her choice of subtitles for *Tehanu*.

> I really thought the story was done; Tenar had finally got her second inning, and Ged and Tenar were obviously happy-ever-after, and if I didn't know exactly who or what Tehanu was, it didn't bother me. But then it began to bother me. And a lot of things about Earthsea were bothering me, like do wizards really have to be celibate, if witches don't? And how come no women at Roke? And who are the dragons? And where do Kargish people go when they die?[12]

These questions and more were answered in *Tales from Earthsea*, a short story collection that helps to fill in some of the gaps in the Earthsea saga. The collection also served to reinterpret some of the concepts from the original trilogy. As an example, witches are generally reviled in the first three books of Earthsea, and the phrase "weak as women's magic" speaks to the low regard in which female practitioners of magic are held. In the story "The Finder," which reveals the origins of the wizarding school on Roke, readers learn that the school was actually *founded* by a coven of female wizards.

In 2001, the same year *Tales from Earthsea* was published, Le Guin also published *The Other Wind*, which is, to date, the last Earthsea book. The book is the story of Alder, a humble sorcerer who is plagued by dreams of death following the sudden passing of his wife, Lily. He fears his dreams may mean that the dead are attempting to breach the stone wall that separates his world from the world of Earthsea. He seeks out Ged, who, along with Tenar, Tehanu, the king of Havnor, and a dragon in human form, travel to Earthsea's most sacred place to make their final stand.

Though the novel does serve as a final chapter in her 40-year-old saga, Le Guin now knows better than to make any promises. When asked about further journeys to Earthsea, she remains noncommittal. "I never know where I'm going next," she said. "Didn't I call the fourth Earthsea book, *Tehanu*, 'The last book of Earthsea'? And then didn't I write two more books of Earthsea? Don't listen to me!"[13]

TO THE FUTURE, VIA THE PAST

In the first decade of the twenty-first century, Le Guin continued to publish frequently, including two short story collections, *The Birthday of the World* (2002) and *Changing Planes* (2003). In 2004, Le Guin released *Gifts*, the first in a three-book series for young readers titled Annals of the Western Shore. The book, and its two sequels, *Voices* (2006) and *Powers* (2007), follow the lives of various characters living in a quasi-medieval world on the western shore of an unspecified country. *Gifts* is the story of Gry, a young girl who can communicate with animals, and Orrec, whose ability to destroy objects with barely a glance is so strong that he has opted to live blindfolded.

In the second book, *Voices*, Gry and Orrec travel to a country in which books have been banned and meet Memer, a girl who has discovered a hidden library that contains the ancient literature of her people. *Powers*, the final book in

Ursula K. Le Guin at home in Portland, Oregon, in 2005. Never content to rest on her laurels, she learned Latin in her seventies to write her 2008 novel, Lavinia, *which won the Locus Award for Best Fantasy Novel.*

the Western Shore saga, tells of Gavir, a slave with the ability to see the future.

Although *Powers* won the Nebula Award for Best Novel in 2008, Le Guin felt that the books in the Western Shore series were not given serious attention from either the science fiction or literary communities, simply because they were labeled as young adult books. "The label YA actually means nothing except that the protagonists, or some of them, are young," she said. "Publishers like it because it is a secure marketing niche. But the cost of security is exclusion from literary consideration. The walls of disdain around any book perceived as being 'for children' are much higher than they were when I began publishing the Earthsea books, forty years ago."[14]

LEARNING LATIN

In 2008, Le Guin published *Lavinia*, perhaps her most ambitious work to date, which was inspired by a character in the ancient epic poem *The Aeneid* by Virgil, whose name is alternately spelled Vergil. She recalled:

> In my 70s I decided it really was time that I really learned Latin, which I'd partly learned and forgotten twice. . . . And I had never got enough Latin into my head to read Virgil, and by then I realized that to read Virgil you kind of have to read him in Latin, he's one of those untranslatable fellas. So I just started my Latin all over again. . . . I started with Virgil's *Eclogues* . . . and then I finally started in the *Aeneid*. Reading maybe ten lines a day, one reads very closely. I'm a fast, careless reader in my own language, and in Latin I'm a very slow, careful reader, and the book simply had an overwhelming effect on me.[15]

Lavinia is the daughter of King Latinus who marries Aeneas, the epic's hero, at the poem's end. A comparatively minor character in Virgil's original work, she was nevertheless a character Le Guin became intrigued by and decided to expand upon. "She's the mother of Rome," she explained. "So I got thinking, what did she think about all this? They're both of them being pushed around by oracles, and destiny, and we know what Aeneas thinks about it, but we don't know what she thought. So she became a character in my mind, and then she started talking to me, the way characters do, that have a story to tell. From then on it was just listening."[16]

Le Guin's novel is divided into two distinct parts. The first is a retelling of *The Aeneid*, while the second picks up where Virgil's text leaves off. "The last part, where I had to go on after Vergil, was very scary to approach," she said.

> [Vergil] really was my guide through the story up till then (just as he was Lavinia's). Now, like Lavinia, all I had to go on were some vague prophecies, and my own sense of what "ought" to happen. This is something novels can do, which drama and epic usually cannot: following up on what happens AFTER the tragedy. How life goes on. This is why a lot of great novels seem a little flat at the end; ending things really isn't their business.[17]

Lavinia not only received the Locus Award, an award presented by the science fiction magazine *Locus*, for Best Fantasy Novel, but the novel also earned Le Guin some of the best reviews of her career. *Entertainment Weekly* called the book "elegant and eloquent," while Jay Parini wrote in the *Los Angeles Times*, "Everywhere Le Guin catches the rhythms of the great epic, echoes them, riffs. In a way, this is a jazzy book, playing in odd syncopation with a massive canonical work. . . . I found myself delighted, even stunned, by the freshness of Le Guin's prose."[18]

BATTLING THE GUILD

On October 21, 2009, Ursula K. Le Guin turned 80 years old. While others her age have long retired, she continued to work, publishing a translation of the *Tao Te Ching* that very year. She also remains an active voice in the literary community. In December 2009, she made news headlines around the world when she resigned from the Author's Guild after almost 40 years of membership. The resignation came in protest of the Author Guild's settlement with Google, the terms of which will allow the search engine to scan and digitize thousands of copyrighted books, making them readily available through a simple search. In a strongly worded letter, Le Guin chastised the Guild for the settlement. "You decided to deal with the devil, as it were, and have presented your arguments for doing so," she wrote. "I wish I could accept them. I can't. There are principles involved, above all the whole concept of copyright; and these you have seen fit to abandon to a corporation, on their terms, without a struggle."[19]

In a letter of response, the Guild defended its position, explaining that, had it attempted to sue Google and

Did you know...

Le Guin has continued to battle the Author's Guild regarding the Google Settlement. On January 25, 2010, she submitted a petition to Judge Denny Chin, who presided over the case between Google and the Author's Guild, demanding that the terms of the settlement be reviewed and that the government be urged "to allow no corporation to circumvent copyright law." As of late January 2010, more than 300 authors had signed the petition in support of Le Guin's cause.

lost, then anyone with a Web site could have conceivably uploaded books, meaning countless books would be on the Internet with no one being held accountable. "Authors would have no say in those uses and no control over the security of those scans," the Guild wrote. "The damage to copyright protection would have been incalculable."[20]

Nevertheless, Le Guin has continued to speak out against the settlement and has attempted to rally other writers to her cause. On the blog Book View Café, Le Guin placed a post hoping to drum up more support for writers looking to speak out against the settlement. "How, where, can I ask writers who are unhappy with the Settlement to speak up— to stand up and be counted?" she wrote.

> We don't have to agree on every detail, but I think there are a lot of us who see it as urgently important to let it be known that writers support the principle of copyright, and want the Copyright Office, the judges, the publishers, and the libraries to know that we intend to keep control of our work, in print or out, printed or electronic, believing that the people who do the work, rather than any corporation, should have the major voice in how it's used and who profits from it.[21]

Despite all of her achievements, fame, and fortune, Le Guin remains grounded, still living a quiet life in Portland. Of all her blessings, she says that she is most grateful for her readers. "A writer without readers is a miserable creature," she explains.

> If you are happy reading my books, believe me, I'm happy that you read them! And happy that you and I meet thus, in a mysterious way—the only true magic I know—in the space of literature, where minds and imaginations meet, and join, and play together, and (even though we are forever strangers—even though we speak different languages) we understand each other.[22]

CHRONOLOGY

1929 Born Ursula Kroeber on October 21 in Berkeley, California.

1947 Attends Radcliffe College in Cambridge, Massachusetts.

1951 Graduates Radcliffe and enters Columbia University in New York City.

1953 Travels to Paris on a Fulbright Fellowship. Marries Charles Le Guin in Paris on December 25.

1954 Teaches French at Mercer University in Macon, Georgia.

1957 Daughter, Elisabeth, is born.

1959 With her husband, moves to Portland, Oregon. Daughter Caroline is born.

1960 Her father, Alfred Kroeber, dies.

1962 Le Guin's first story, "April in Paris," is published in the magazine *Fantastic Stories of Imagination*.

1964 Son, Theodore, is born.

1966 *Rocannon's World* and *Planet of Exile* are both published in the same year.

1967 *City of Illusion* is published.

1968 *A Wizard of Earthsea* is published.

1969 *The Left Hand of Darkness* is published and wins a Nebula Award.

1970 Le Guin wins the Hugo Award for *The Left Hand of Darkness*.

1971 Publishes *The Lathe of Heaven* and the second Earthsea book, *The Tombs of Atuan*.

1972 *The Tombs of Atuan* wins Le Guin a Newbery Honor Book Citation. *The Farthest Shore*, the third Earthsea book, is published and wins the National Book Award for Children's Literature.

1973 Wins a Hugo Award for her novella, *The Word for World Is Forest*.

1974 *The Dispossessed* is published and wins the Nebula and Jupiter awards.

1975 Le Guin publishes the poetry collection, *Wild Angels*, and the short story collection, *The Wind's Twelve Quarters*. *The Dispossessed* wins the Hugo Award.

1976 *Very Far Away From Anywhere Else* and *Orsinian Tales* are published.

1977 Le Guin edits *Nebula Award Stories Eleven*, a collection of award-winning science fiction stories.

1978 *The Eye of the Heron* is published.

1979 *The Language of the Night*, a collection of essays, is published.

1980 The film adaptation of *The Lathe of Heaven* airs on PBS. *The Beginning Place* is published.

1982 The short story collection, *The Compass Rose*, is published.

1983 Gives the commencement address at Mills College in Oakland, California.

1984 *Solomon Leviathan's Nine Hundred and Thirty-First Trip Around the World*, a book for children, is published.

1985 *Always Coming Home* is published.

1988 *Catwings*, the first book in the series, is published.

1989 *Dancing at the Edge of the World*, an essay collection, is published, as is the second Catwings book, *Catwings Return*.

1990 *Tehanu: The Last Book of Earthsea* is published and wins the Nebula Award.

1991 *Searoad* is published. *Tehanu* wins a Locus Award.

1992 Two more books for children, *Fish Soup* and *A Ride on the Red Mare's Back*, are published.

1994 The short story collection, *A Fisherman of the Inland Sea*, is published. *Wonderful Alexander and the Catwings* is published.

1995 *Four Ways to Forgiveness* is published.

1996 The short story collection, *Unlocking the Air and Other Stories*, is published.

1998 *Steering the Craft*, a book on writing, is published.

1999 *Jane on Her Own*, the fourth Catwings book, is published.

2000 Receives the Library of Congress' "Living Legends" award in the category "Writers and Artists." *The Telling* is published.

2001 *The Telling* wins a Locus Award. *Tales from Earthsea* and *The Other Wind*, the fifth and sixth books of Earthsea, are published.

2002 A second TV adaptation of *The Lathe of Heaven* airs on A&E. The short story collection, *The Birthday of the World*, is published.

2003 The short story collection, *Changing Planes*, is published.

2004 Le Guin is a named a Mary Hill Arbuthnot Honor Lecturer for the Association for Library Service to Children. She also wins the Margaret A. Edwards Award for her lifetime contribution to young adult literature. *Legends of Earthsea* airs on the Sci-Fi Channel (now SyFy). *Gifts* is published.

2005 *Gifts* wins a PEN Center USA Award for children's literature. *Tales from Earthsea*, an animated film from Goro Miyazaki, is released.

2006 *Voices*, the second book in the Annals of the Western Shore, is released. Le Guin wins the Maxine Cushing Gray Award at the Seattle Public Library.

2007 *Powers*, the third book in the Annals of the Western Shore, is released.

2008 *Powers* wins the Nebula Award. *Lavinia* is published.

2009 *Cheek by Jowl*, a collection of essays, is published. Le Guin resigns from the Author's Guild in protest over the Google Settlement, which will allow books to be scanned and downloaded via the Internet.

NOTES

Chapter 1

1 Ursula K. Le Guin and Susan Wood, ed., *Language of the Night: Essays on Fantasy and Science Fiction*. New York: Berkeley, 1979, p. 57.

2 Leonard S. Marcus, *The Wand in the Word: Conversations with Writers of Fantasy*. Cambridge: Candlewick Press, 2006, p. 94.

3 Guy Haley, "Ursula K. Le Guin: The *Death Ray* Interview," *Death Ray*, October 2007.

4 Carl Freedman, ed., *Conversations with Ursula K. Le Guin*, Jackson, Miss.: University Press of Mississippi, 2008, p. 49.

5 Theresa Hogue, "Q&A with Author Ursula K. Le Guin," *Gazette-Times*, September 12, 2008.

6 Freedman, *Conversations with Ursula K. Le Guin*, p. 47.

Chapter 2

1 Cindy Heidemann, *Lifetime Achievement Award*, Pacific Northwest Booksellers Association, 2001.

2 Marcus, *The Wand in the Word: Conversations with Writers of Fantasy*, p. 92.

3 Elizabeth Cummins, ed., *Understanding Ursula K. Le Guin*, Columbia, S.C.: University of South Carolina Press, 1993, p. 2.

4 Ursula K. Le Guin, *Dancing at the Edge of the World*. New York: Grove Press, 1989, p. 140.

5 Haley, "Ursula K. Le Guin: The *Death Ray* Interview."

6 Theodora Kroeber, *Alfred Kroeber: A Personal Configuration*. Berkeley: University of California Press, 1970, p. 141.

7 Ibid.

8 Scott Timberg, "Ursula K. Le Guin's Work Still Resonates with Readers, *Los Angeles Times*, May 10, 2009. http://www.latimes.com=features=books=la-ca-ursula-leguin10-2009may10,0,3098697.story.

9 Marcus, *The Wand in the Word: Conversations with Writers of Fantasy*, p. 94.

10 Marcus, *The Wand in the Word: Conversations with Writers of Fantasy*, p. 93.

11 Ibid.

12 Steve LaFreniere, "Ursula K. LeGuin," *Vice*. http://www.viceland.com/int/v15n12/htdocs/ursula-k-le-guin-440.php.

13 Timberg, "Ursula K. Le Guin's Still Resonates with Readers."

14 Ursula K. Le Guin, "Lord Dunsany: *In the Land of Time and Other Fantasy Tales:* A Review by Ursula K Le Guin." http://www.ursulakleguin.com/UKL-Review-Joshi-LordDunsany.html.

15 Barbara J. Bucknall, *Ursula K. Le Guin*. New York: Fredrick Ungar Publishing Co., 1981, p. 3.

Chapter 3

1 Marcus, *The Wand in the Word: Conversations with Writers of Fantasy*, p. 96.

2 Ibid., p. 9.

3 Harold Bloom, ed., *Ursula K. Le Guin*, New York: Chelsea House, 1986, p. 119.

4 Freedman, *Conversations with Ursula K. Le Guin*, p. 105.

5 Ursula K. Le Guin, "Frequently Asked Questions." http://www.ursulakleguin.com/FAQ.html.

6 Marcus, *The Wand in the Word: Conversations with Writers of Fantasy*, p. 96.

7 Le Guin and Wood, *The Language of the Night*, p. 27.

8 Ibid., p. 28.

9 Ibid.

Chapter 4

1 Haley, "Ursula K. Le Guin: The *Death Ray* Interview."

2 Bloom, *Ursula K. Le Guin*, p. 187.

3 Ibid.

4 Bucknall, *Ursula K. Le Guin*, p. 71.

5 Haley, "Ursula K. Le Guin: The *Death Ray* Interview."

6 Le Guin and Wood, *Language of the Night*, pp. 140–141.

7 Le Guin and Wood, *Language of the Night*, pp. 140–141.

8 Freedman, *Conversations with Ursula K. Le Guin*, p. 18.

Chapter 5

1 Le Guin and Wood, *Language of the Night*, p. 51.

2 Ibid.

3 Ibid., p. 50.

4 Ibid., p. 51.

5 Ibid.

6 Ibid., pp. 49–50.

7 "Chronicles of Earthsea," *Guardian* (London), February 9, 2004. http://www.guardian.co.uk/books/2004/feb/09/sciencefiction fantasyandhorror.ursulakleguin.

8 Le Guin and Wood, *Language of the Night*, p. 52.

9 Ibid.

10 Ibid., p. 63.

11 Ursula K. Le Guin, "A Whitewashed Earthsea," Slate.com. http://www.slate.com/id/2111107/.

12 Ibid.

13 Haley, "Ursula K. Le Guin: The *Death Ray* Interview."

14 Ibid.

15 Le Guin, "A Whitewashed Earthsea."

16 Ursula K. Le Guin, "Gedo Senki." http://www.ursulakleguin.com/GedoSenkiResponse.html.

17 Haley, "Ursula K. Le Guin: The *Death Ray* Interview."

Chapter 6

1 Le Guin, *Dancing at the Edge of the World*, p. 171.

2 Ibid., pp. 9–10.

Chapter 7

1 Le Guin and Wood, *Language of the Night*, pp. 29–30.

2 Philip K. Dick, "Man, Android and Machine," Grey Lodge Occult Review. http://www.greylodge.org/occultreview/glor_004/manandroid.htm.

3 Freedman, ed., *Conversations with Ursula K. Le Guin*, p. 55.

4 Le Guin, *Dancing at the Edge of the World*, p. 125.

5 Ursula K. Le Guin, *The Lathe of Heaven*, New York: Scribner, 1971, p. 26.

6 Carl Freedman, ed., p. 132.

7 Ibid., p. 45.

8 Le Guin, *Dancing at the Edge of the World*, p. 36.

9 Ibid., p. 31.

10 Michael Speier, "The Lathe of Heaven," *Daily Variety*, September 5, 2002.

11 Freedman, ed., *Conversations with Ursula K. Le Guin*, p. 57.

12 Ibid., p. 45.

13 Le Guin and Wood, *Language of the Night*, p. 153.

14 Freedman, ed., *Conversations with Ursula K. Le Guin*, p. 133.

15 Ibid., p. 101.

16 Ibid., p. 124.

17 Le Guin and Wood, *Language of the Night*, p. 55.

18 Ibid.

19 Ibid., p. 30.

Chapter 8

1 Freedman, ed., *Conversations with Ursula K. Le Guin*, p. 15.

2 Ibid., p. 125.

3 Ibid., p. 34.

Chapter 9

1 Freedman, ed., *Conversations with Ursula K. Le Guin*, p. 150.

2 Ibid., p. 63.

3 Ibid., pp. 143–144.

4 Ibid., p. 151.

5 Ibid.

6 Ibid., p. 130.

7 Mike Cadden, *Ursula K. Le Guin: Beyond Genre, Fiction for Children and Adults*, New York and London: Routledge, 2005, p. 161.

8 Orson Scott Card, "Books to Look For," *Fantasy and Science Fiction*, December 1991.

9 Mike Cadden, *Ursula K. Le Guin: Beyond Genre*, p. 160.

10 Ibid.

Chapter 10

1 Chieko Akaishi, "Ursula K. Le Guin," *Femin*. http://www.jca.apc.org/femin/gmk/leguin_original.html.

2 Ibid.

3 Steve LaFreniere, "Ursula K. LeGuin," *Vice*. http://www.viceland.com/int/v15n12/htdocs/ursula-k-le-guin-440.php.

4 Freedman, ed., *Conversations with Ursula K. Le Guin*, p. 121.

5 Ibid., p. 173.

6 Ibid., p. 116.

7 Ibid., p. 117.

8 Ibid., p. 86.

9 Ibid., p. 117.

10 Ursula K. Le Guin, *The Wave in the Mind*, Boston: Shambhala, 2004, p. 279.

11 Cindy Heidemann, "Ursula K. Le Guin: Lifetime Achievement Award," pnba.org. http://www.pnba.org/ursula.htm.

12 Ursula K. Le Guin, "The Other Wind." http://www.ursulakleguin.com/OtherWind_Note.html.

13 Theresa Hogue, "Q&A with author Ursula K. Le Guin," *Corvallis Gazette-Times*, September 12, 2008. http://www.gazettetimes.com/news/local/article_e6294917-5fa7-5c83-a0b2-f912539017d7.html.

14 Alexander Chee, "Breaking into the Spell," *Guernica Magazine*. http://www.guernicamag.com=interviews=505=breaking_into_the_spell_1=.

15 Transcript of an interview with Le Guin on *The Book Show*. http://www.abc.net.au/rn/bookshow/stories/2008/2221112.htm.

16 Lev Grossman, "An Interview with Ursula K. Le Guin," techland.com. http://techland.com/2009/05/11/an-interview-with-ursula-k-le-guin/.

17 "Sing Muse, of the Woman Unsung," *The Inkwell Review*. http://inkwellreview.blogspot.com/2008/06/sing-muse-of-woman-unsung.html.

18 Jay Parini, *Los Angeles Times*. http://www.ursulakleguin.com/Index-Lavinia.html.

19 Ursula K. Le Guin, "My Resignation from the Authors Guild." http://www.ursulakleguin.com/Note-AGResignation.html.

20 "Ursula K. Le Guin, Google, and the Economics of Authorship." http://www.authorsguild.org/advocacy/articles/ursula-k-le-guin-google-and.html.

21 E.B. Boyd, ". . .And Ursula K. Le Guin Starts Saber-Rattling," Baynewser, January 12, 2010. http://www.mediabistro.com=baynewser=google_book_settlement/.

22 Alejandro Serrano, "Fantasymundo Interview with Ursula K. Le Guin," Fantasymundo.com, May 2, 2008. http://www.fantasymundo.com/articulos/1157/fantasymundo_entrevista_ursula_k_guin_terramar.

WORKS BY URSULA K. LE GUIN

1966 *Rocannon's World; Planet of Exile*

1967 *City of Illusion*

1968 *A Wizard of Earthsea*

1969 *The Left Hand of Darkness*

1970 *The Tombs of Atuan*

1971 *The Lathe of Heaven; The Tombs of Athan*

1972 *The Farthest Shore; The Word for World is Forest*

1974 *The Dispossessed*

1975 *The Wind's Twelve Quarters; Wild Angels*

1976 *Very Far Away From Anywhere Else; Orsinian Tales*

1979 *Malafrena; The Language of the Night; Leese Webster*

1980 *The Beginning Place*

1983 *The Eye of The Heron; The Compass Rose*

1985 *Always Coming Home*

1987 *Buffalo Gals*

1988 *Catwings*

1989 *Catwings Return; Dancing at the Edge of the World*

1990 *Tehanu: The Last Book of Earthsea*

1991 *Searoad*

1992 *A Ride on the Red Mare's Back; Fish Soup*

1994 *Wonderful Alexander and the Catwings; A Fisherman of the Inland Sea*

1995 *Four Ways to Forgiveness*

1996 *Unlocking the Air and Other Stories*

1998 *Steering the Craft*

1999 *Jane on Her Own*

2000 *The Telling*

2001 *Tales from Earthsea; The Other Wind*

2002 *The Birthday of the World; Tom Mouse*
2003 *Changing Planes*
2004 *Gifts*
2006 *Voices*
2007 *Powers*
2008 *Lavinia*
2009 *Cheek by Jowl*

POPULAR BOOKS

THE DISPOSSESSED

A scientist living in an anarchic planet travels to its capitalistic sister world on a mission of discovery that opens up his mind to the shortcomings of both worlds.

THE LATHE OF HEAVEN

In early twenty-first century Portland, Oregon, a man whose dreams become reality finds himself at the whim of an unscrupulous scientist who wishes to harness that power for his own ends.

THE LEFT HAND OF DARKNESS

An envoy from Earth arrives on a snowy planet in hopes of welcoming its citizens into joining his culture. Along the way he becomes embroiled in a political power struggle and makes a remarkable journey of discovery with an alien who can change genders.

A WIZARD OF EARTHSEA

A young boy discovers he possesses magical abilities and hones his craft at a school for wizardry. While there, he unleashes a malevolent shadow that follows him relentlessly.

POPULAR CHARACTERS

GED

The hero of the Earthsea books, Ged begins his life as a young wizard sent to the wizarding school on the island of Roke and grows into a powerful sorcerer who makes a great sacrifice to save his world.

GENLY AI

A traveler from the Ekumen who becomes entangled in a political struggle on the snow-driven planet of Winter. He becomes friends with Estraven, an alien who can change genders.

GEORGE ORR

Orr is a mild-mannered draftsman whose dreams have the power to become reality. His power is abused by William Haber, a psychiatrist who wishes to use George's abilities to make himself more powerful.

SHEVEK

A scientist living on Anarres, a moon of the planet Urras, he leaves his home world to travel to Urras and undergoes a powerful awakening regarding the differences and similarities between the two cultures.

TENAR

A priestess first introduced in the second Earthsea book, *The Tombs of Atuan*, she becomes the wife of Ged and the two form a powerful bond as they work together to save Earthsea from destruction.

MAJOR AWARDS

1969 Le Guin wins the Nebula Award and the Hugo Award for *The Left Hand of Darkness*.

1972 She wins the Newbery Silver Medal Award for *The Tombs of Atuan* and the National Book Award for Children's Books for *The Farthest Shore*.

1973 Le Guin wins the Hugo Award for *The Word for World Is Forest* and the Locus Award for *The Lathe of Heaven*.

1974 She wins the Hugo Award for her short story, "The Ones Who Walk Away from Omelas."

1975 Le Guin wins the Nebula Award for her short story, "The Day Before the Revolution," and the Nebula Award and the Hugo Award for *The Dispossessed*.

1979 She wins the Lewis Carroll Shelf Award for *A Wizard of Earthsea* and a Gandalf Award.

1988 Le Guin wins the Hugo Award for her short story, "Buffalo Gals."

1990 She wins the Nebula Award for *Tehanu*.

1992 Le Guin is shortlisted for the Pulitzer Prize for *Searoad*.

2001 She wins a Lifetime Achievement Award from the Pacific Northwest Booksellers Association.

2003 Le Guin is named a Grand Master of the Science Fiction Writers Association.

2009 She wins the Locus Award for Best Fantasy Novel for *Lavinia*.

BIBLIOGRAPHY

Bucknall, Barbara J. *Ursula K. Le Guin*. New York: Fredrick Ungar Publishing Co., 1981.

Freedman, Carl, ed. *Conversations with Ursula K. Le Guin*. Jackson, Miss.: University Press of Mississippi, 2008.

Le Guin, Ursula and Wood, Susan, ed. *Language of the Night: Essays on Fantasy and Science Fiction*. New York: Berkeley, 1979.

Marcus, Leonard S. *The Wand in the Word: Conversations with Writers of Fantasy*. Cambridge: Candlewick Press, 2006.

FURTHER READING

Books

Bloom, Harold, ed. *Ursula K. Le Guin*. New York: Chelsea House, 1986.

De Bolt, Joe, ed. *Ursula K. Le Guin: Voyager to Inner Lands and to Outer Space*. Port Washington, N.Y.: Kennikat Press, 1979.

Le Guin, Ursula K. *Dancing at the Edge of the World: Thoughts on Words, Women, Places*. New York: Grove Press, 1989.

————. *The Wave in the Mind: Talks and Essays on the Writer, the Reader, and the Imagination*. Boston: Shambhala, 2004.

Web Sites

Ursula K. Le Guin—Official Website
http://www.ursulakleguin.com

PICTURE CREDITS

INDEX

ABOUT THE CONTRIBUTOR

JEREMY K. BROWN has written for numerous magazines and publications, including *Star*, *Country Music Today*, *Wizard*, *Current Biography*, and *WWE Magazine*. He is the author of the biography *Stevie Wonder*, the editor of the reference book *Warfare in the 21st Century*, and has published numerous short stories. He lives in New York with his wife and family.